When The Other Shoe Falls

By
Maureen Gavin

1stBooks – rev. 01/25/01

Chapter One

The earth stood still one day in April, 1952, and I got on for the ride. I believe from that day forward, I was the world's most optimistic pessimist. With the first smack on the ass from the doctor I knew life was going to be bitter-sweet. After all, the doctor had just forced me to take my first breath and he caused me pain in the process.

All the old adages have their merit; if life gives you lemons, make lemonade; when one door closes, another one opens; it is better to have loved and lost, than never to have loved. You get the idea. But it has been my experience that as soon as you think things are going fine — wham — someone or something is going to knock you down a few pegs to prove they're not. Thus, my explanation of being an optimistic pessimist; if you always expect the very worst, then you won't be disappointed when it happens; and you'll be pleasantly surprised when it doesn't.

I was the third and last daughter of my parents. My grandmother informed my mother when I was two months old that I was "special." This is not to suggest that I was her favorite because my cousin, Anne, already had that honor; she only sensed something in me that the others did not have. Mom thought Granny was being sarcastic because all I did for those first two months was cry. This was the reason, I was told all my life, why I was my parents' last child. Mom feared that if she continued to have any more children, they would progressively get worse. This logic stems from the fact that their first child was an angel. They could wake her up in the middle of a nap to show her off to company, then put her back to bed with no problem. The second one was not quite as cooperative. She would go to bed nicely, but couldn't be "shown off" without fussing later. So when I came along and cried day and night, my parents took to tiptoeing around when I finally did shut up long enough to sleep. Ergo, number four could only promise a life of complete misery. So what Granny meant by "special" wasn't clarified until many years later.

My sister, Nancy, is five years older than I am, and Retta is two years older. We had the usual sibling rivalry any family with more than one child has growing up. But Nancy always said that when we grew up, we would live together as old ladies. I never knew why she felt this way because Retta and I were closer in age and we had more in common with each other. We played the same games and had the same friends, while Nancy had a different set of friends who were just a bit older than us.

I formed a closeness with each of my sisters at different ages. I remember when Retta was ten; she fell into a partially frozen lake while we were bravely trying to see if it was solid. It wasn't. She fell in only to her knees, but I screamed loud enough to be heard a block away when the ice cracked. I started to cry because I thought Retta was going to die. She started to laugh, and I cried harder because I still feared for her life. I was always told that if you fell into a lake that wasn't completely frozen, you would die.

2

My belief almost came true when we got home. Mom saw Retta soaking wet and damn near killed her. She threw her into a hot bathtub and had to leave the room because she felt like drowning her herself for being so stupid as to walk on a lake that wasn't fully frozen. I didn't understand Mom's reaction. I couldn't figure out why she was so pissed off that Retta was still alive.

Nancy, however, had good reason to grow up hating her obnoxious little sister. When Dad had to drive Nancy and her first date to the homecoming dance in her freshman year of high school, he had the lack of foresight to bring me along for the ride. I remember sitting in the front seat of the car with Dad and hanging over into the back seat so I could ask her escort, "Did you know that you're the first boy Nancy's ever dated?" I saw her cheeks turn red in embarrassment, and I kept trying to make it worse with every word I said. Dad finally smacked me on the butt and told me to sit down and shut up. As he was fully aware, sitting down and shutting up were things I hadn't mastered. My mouth has many times gotten me in trouble and sometimes I have paid dearly.

In spite of this, we remain close even now. When we were older, and Retta had a boyfriend who could drive, we used to go to Brigantine, a shore resort town only an hour's drive from our home in Turnersville, New Jersey. Jack, Retta's boyfriend, enjoyed taking all three of us to the shore because he looked like Mr. Studley with his own harem. In fact, once Retta got a job as a hairdresser, Jack continued to take Nancy and me to Brigantine for the day while Retta stayed home and worked on Saturdays. Some people thought that odd, but Nancy and I considered Jack the brother we never had. That worked out well, since Retta and Jack got married a year after high school graduation, and he did become our brother.

When Retta and Jack had their first child, a boy also named Jack, Nancy and I claimed him as our own. We both still lived at home, so if Retta needed a sitter while she worked on Saturdays, we'd actually fight over who got to baby-sit. We'd take him everywhere with us and brag about how perfect he was to everyone who'd listen.

That was the summer of 1969, and I started to work as well. I got my first job as a cashier in a supermarket at the age seventeen. I lied on the application, claiming to be eighteen, because no one would hire me if I wasn't. It was while I worked at that supermarket that I truly had my right of passage. I lost my virginity there, in more ways than one.

Chapter Two

Two of my best girlfriends had steady boyfriends and had already been sexually active. I had not found "Mr. Right," so I had not been. When prom time came around, they both had their steady dates to go with. I, however, had to ask my cousin, Jerry, to take me. No one knew Jerry, so we passed ourselves off as boyfriend and girlfriend for the night. I was a senior and Jerry was a "big man on campus" from Villanova, so my girlfriends were suitably impressed.

The problem arose when my girlfriend, Connie, asked Jerry and me to double with her and her boyfriend, Bill. I said okay, and that was the beginning of one of the most uncomfortable nights of my life. Bill was the driver for the night, and he decided that he wanted to go parking after the prom. This would probably not have been a problem if Jerry had really been the boyfriend I had portrayed him to be. But it soon became evident that something wasn't right.

Bill drove to the lover's lookout point and proceeded to make out with Connie in the front seat. Jerry and I were in the back, and all we could do was talk — incest not being the night's objective. After some time, I heard Bill say to Connie, "Doesn't she ever shut up? What did we come here for anyway?"

5

Jerry and I both laughed and continued to talk, much to Bill's frustration. He decided to start the car, and we called it a night. Years later, at a class reunion, I finally told Connie and Bill — who were married by then — why I sat and talked with Jerry for the entire night. It made for a good laugh.

Losing one's virginity can happen physically only once. However, being very naive at seventeen years old, I found out that the big world out there causes a certain loss of innocence as well.

As I said before, I started working when I was a senior in high school. I used to take the bus from school and go directly to work in my Catholic school uniform. Harry, my Jewish boss, decided that I should wear a smock because he didn't want my "religious statement" to offend his customers. He, however, always wore short sleeved dress shirts which showed the tattooed numbers on his arm from when he was imprisoned during the war in the death camps.

Everyone was always saddened to hear how he lost his entire family in the camps and was left with nothing when he came to this country in 1948. I was sympathetic as well until I got to know him. No matter what he experienced, an obnoxious person is an obnoxious person. He had vowed that he would never again be persecuted, and he set out to "fuck the world before it fucks me again".

Harry had gone into partnership with another man when he bought this store. The two of them were as different as night and day. Harry was the personification of evil and greed, while Lou was a sweet old man with a bad cigar habit. Lou treated the girls like his granddaughters, and Harry treated us like his slaves, and worse.

I was only working there for about one month when Harry came up to me during a break and stuck his tongue in my ear. I was appalled and frightened at the same time.

He reached down to grab my breast and said to me, "Darling, I want to fuck you."

I pushed his hand away and ran out of the breakroom. I went back to my register and started to work just to get away from him. The term "sexual harassment" did not exist in 1969, so I didn't know I could do anything about it. I was afraid of him and thought I was the only one this happened to.

Not long after, though, I heard him say to another cashier, "Darling, I'll put a fifty dollar bill under each of your cheeks if you let me fuck you."

I felt both relief and disgust when I heard that. At least it wasn't only me. I asked this woman if he did this to everybody.

She told me he did; it was "his way."

I said, "I guess I'd better grow up because I didn't know that this is what goes on in the workplace."

She, being older than I, said, "Honey, Harry is a man like no other. This is not normal, and don't assume it is. He's a pig, but I need the job, so I listen to his crap and go home to my husband. He's all talk, so just take it and ignore it."

So, for the next nine years, while I finished high school, college, and my first four years of marriage, I listened to Harry talk about fucking every female who had the misfortune of working for him. No one was safe from his vulgarity.

I first fell in love in this store and, needless to say, it wasn't with Harry. I was working there for a year and had become friendly with many other employees. One was

7

Carl, the store manager. He was thirty-three years old, married, and had two children. He was "little boy cute". He had jet black hair, and light blue eyes. His cheeks dimpled when he smiled. He had a great sense of humor, and I found myself eager to work on his shift. We became friends, and I enjoyed his company. We would take breaks together and talk. Then, one night, he leaned over and kissed me. It was not a passionate kiss. It was gentle and soft.

I thought my heart would stop. I was surprised and thrilled at the same time. I thought I had to be special if a married man would kiss me. Surely, a married man would never do such a thing unless it was for a good reason. Need I say, my naivete was immense.

Chapter Three

My affair with Carl lasted for two years. I loved Carl like all first loves do, completely and with abandon. The fact that he was married only added to the excitement. I found stolen kisses during our breaks to be exhilarating. We went from that to "dates" at the movies. We drove for an hour to find a theater where none of his married friends would see him. It never occurred to me that we were doing something morally wrong. It was fun, a lark, something different. I never thought of his wife or children. They were not part of our life, so they didn't exist for me.

When the relationship evolved into a sexual one, I was elated. I finally met my "Mr. Right." He was sweet and gentle, and I was in love.

We had been sneaking around for a year and a half when he announced that he was going to leave his wife. He said he wanted to move to California and start over. I was taken aback. First, I had never asked him to leave his wife. Second, I wasn't ready to move to California. I was in my second year of college and looking forward to graduating. If I left then, I knew I would never finish. So, he instead opted to move into a one bedroom apartment over a body shop.

I was happy then because I could date him openly and introduce him to my parents, who were not thrilled with his age or his "estranged" marital status. My father worried that I would fall in love with him and not be able to marry him because Catholics did not recognize divorce. Little did he know that I was already in love with Carl and didn't give a damn about the Catholic opinion of our relationship.

Things started to fall apart shortly after Carl moved out of his house. His twelve year old son kept begging him to come home. His wife never knew I was in the picture and made an offer of reconciliation. He was missing his seven year old daughter's first experiences of learning to read. He was depressed.

My twentieth birthday came around. He took me to a Phillies baseball game. I didn't particularly like baseball, but I knew he did, so I went with him. During the game, he was distant. He didn't seem to want to be there. I felt like I was losing him to his family. I knew where his mind was. I kept asking what was wrong. I sensed that he was about to break up with me to return home. I didn't want to believe it or face it, so I chose not to ask the obvious. He took me home from the game and went back to his apartment.

That was on a Friday. On Monday, I didn't work on his shift, so I didn't see him. On Tuesday, he called me to say he had to go to a meeting with Harry and Lou about store business. He said he would call me when he came back. He never did.

He didn't show up for work for the rest of the week. No one knew where he was. Lou called his wife when he could get no answer at Carl's apartment. She said she hadn't heard form him since Tuesday, before the meeting. Lou didn't tell her that Carl never showed up for the meeting.

I became alarmed that Carl had taken off for California, since he always wanted to start over out there. I drove everywhere we had ever been to look for him and I even called his cousin to see if he had any news about Carl going out west.

On Friday, April 28th, 1972, they found his body. He had hooked a garden hose up to the tailpipe of his car and ran it through a cracked window.

Chapter Four

I was only twenty years old, and I felt like my life was over. My love was gone, and I, too, had nothing more to live for.

Carl's wife, Rita, took care of the funeral arrangements.

All of my co-workers knew of our relationship and were very supportive of me. I took time off from work and fell into a valium-induced stupor. I stopped going to my classes. I did nothing but sleep and cry. My father called my counselor at school and told her about the situation. She informed all of my professors and, thankfully, they allowed me to miss those classes without penalty. I finished the year out, but I don't remember doing it. I was lost.

I found myself spending more and more time at Carl's grave. It soon became summer, and all I wanted to do was lie down on his grave and join him. But one day, I got a message at work from Carl's wife. It said only, "Have Maureen call me."

I was dumbfounded. I had never spoken to her, and I wondered what she could possibly want from me. I even stayed away from the funeral because I didn't feel I should encroach on her in her time of grief or allow her to see the extent of mine. I had no desire to hurt her by letting her know about our relationship prior to his leaving her. However, I called her, as she asked me to.

She said, matter-of-factly, "Maureen, I have something here for you."

I thought, *What? A bullet?*

She said only that she wanted me to come to her house so she could give it to me. The strange thing was, she wanted me to go there at midnight.

I asked, "Why midnight?"

She merely said, "That's the time I want to see you." She never gave me a better reason than that.

So, I agreed. I called my girlfriend, Mary, and told her about the strange request. We both felt something was greatly wrong with that scenario, but Mary said she'd go with me anyway.

Before we drove to Rita's, I stopped at the township police station. I told the night officer where Mary and I were going. Because it was a small town, the officer knew about the suicide. After I explained Rita's request for a midnight meeting, I asked for police protection. I honestly thought that Rita had found out about the relationship and wanted to kill me. It must have sounded feasible to the sergeant because he agreed to follow us in a squad car.

So, Mary and I knocked on the door at midnight.

Rita opened it and invited us in.

I felt extremely uncomfortable walking into Carl's home. I sensed his presence, and it felt strange.

Rita suggested that we join her mother in the kitchen.

Mary and I walked into the room and sat down.

Rita asked, "How long did you know my husband?"

I said, "Three years. We worked together."

She said, "My husband left you a letter."

My heart skipped a beat.

"Can I have it?" I asked.

The doorbell rang.

Imagine my face when I looked over to see the police sergeant standing in the doorway. I had forgotten all about him.

He asked if Mary and I were all right.

"Why wouldn't they be?" asked Rita. She turned back to me, "You actually brought the police with you?"

I smiled weakly at the officer and said, "We're okay. I'm sorry, I forgot you were out there."

Rita said, "They're fine. You can go."

He looked at us, shook his head, and said, "Good night."

Then he left.

Rita came back into the kitchen. "What did you think, that I was going to shoot you or something?"

I said, "Well, it is midnight."

She shook her head. Then she left the room briefly and came back with an envelope. She handed it to me. "I got Carl's car out of the compound today, and he left two letters in the visor. One is addressed to me, and the other is addressed to you."

The envelope was already opened. I knew she had read it. My hands shook as I opened it. I felt myself start to cry, and I hoped with all my might that the tears would not fall in front of Rita. I read the letter.

Maureen,

I'm sorry it has to be this way. I wish it culd have ended different. But I culdn't go to the meeting today and be fired by Harry with Lou their. I can't face anybody anymore. I wish things culd have worked out. But they can't. Remember I always love you.

Love always,
Carl

I'm still amazed that, through the fog of tears, all I could see was his misspelling and bad grammar. I was in a state of shock. I saw the "Love always" and handed the letter to Mary. She read it and gave it back to me.

I knew then, from his own words, that his fear of being fired "today" meant that he had been dead since April 25th. He hadn't been found until the 28th, when two kids playing ball came upon his car at the edge of the woods. I re-read the words until Rita's mother ripped the letter from my hands.

"You harlot," she screamed.

Where's a good cop when you need one? I thought.

Rita told her mother to sit down and gently took the letter away from her. She said to me, "How did you have time to see Carl? He was home all the time. The only time he ever went out was on Tuesday nights to his card game."

I couldn't believe she was still so blind. She hadn't even figured out that I had been the Tuesday night card game for the past two years. I couldn't bring myself to say, "You fool, there were no card games," so I feebly said, "I saw him at work."

She seemed to buy that.

I asked her for the letter again.

She said, "No, this is one of the last things he wrote. I want to keep it. You can read it again, but it stays here. I just wanted to see you, to see what he saw in you." Then she once again handed me the letter.

I etched it into my mind, bad spelling and all, so I could rewrite the words when I got outside. I never wanted to lose his last thoughts. Finally, I passed the letter back to Rita.

After that, Mary and I stood to leave. On our way out I saw Carl's son in the hallway. He looked at me, and then he ran down the hall to his room. I felt horrible. Carl's home, Carl's wife, Carl's son. The whole scene overwhelmed me. I pulled the door open, and Mary and I left.

When we got to the car, I quickly opened the glove compartment, found paper, and wrote the words from the letter. I sat there and cried as Mary drove us back to her house. I stayed at Mary's house the rest of the night. I clutched my version of the letter all night long. I had mixed emotions. I felt bad for whatever part I may have played in his family's pain. I also felt good, knowing that he had me in his thoughts before his final breath was taken.

I never returned to his grave after that night.

Chapter Five

For the next few months, all I did was walk through life without living it. My friends tried to get me out of the house to do things, and I did them, but all by rote. I remember nothing at all about those months, except for the pain I felt. I'd hear a song on the radio and cry. It was uncontrollable. I hated living.

Finally, the first anniversary of Carl's death came around. I knew that I did not want to go to work or even stay in my own house that weekend. My family was concerned about my mental state, and I couldn't stand to see the pity in their faces. It made me feel worse. So, when a friend of Nancy's said she was going to Atlantic City for a "Singles Weekend," I asked if I could join her. I wanted to be where no one knew me and where no one would ask, "Are you okay?"

On a very rainy Friday night, Carol and I took off for the shore. It took almost two hours to make the normally forty-five minute ride because of a virtual monsoon. We had to stop twice on the way because we couldn't see through the windshield. But we finally got there at around ten-thirty, two and a half hours after the party in the bar had started.

I was determined to have a good time that weekend. I didn't want to feel sorry for myself any longer. I was with people who did not know about Carl. It made the night easier.

Carol and I got around the room and talked to several people. She introduced me to two friends of hers, Joe and Pete. They bought us each a drink, and Pete took turns dancing with us, while Joe sat at the bar and watched.

The room became full, and the air conditioning didn't seem like it was working. I switched to ginger ale, since I found myself getting too hot and drinking too much.

It was hours later when I passed out from the heat. I had never fainted before, so I didn't recognize the feeling I had before I hit the floor. When I came to, a waitress had a wet towel on my forehead. I looked up into the spinning ball in the center of the dance floor. I thought, my God, everybody's going to think I'm a drunk. I stood up immediately and apologized to the waitress. "I'm sorry. I'm not a drunk, really. Please believe me."

She laughed and said, "Honey, a drunk doesn't get up that fast. It's the heat. Go sit down, and you'll be fine."

Carol was nowhere to be found, so I went and sat down in a nearby booth.

She finally made her way over to me after Joe said to her, "You better go check your girlfriend, she just took a dive on the dance floor."

"Are you okay?" she asked.

"Yeah, I just fainted. It must be the heat. I'm going up to the room."

She opted to stay and party some more.

I left. I wasn't in the room long when I heard a knock at the door. I thought that Carol had changed her mind, but I opened the door to find Joe standing there with two cups of coffee and a tray of doughnuts.

"I'm not a drunk, really," I said.

He laughed, "I didn't say you were. Want something to eat?"

I motioned for him to come in.

He walked over to the table and put the coffee and doughnuts down.

I was slightly uncomfortable because I was in a hotel room with a man I just met. There we were, sitting at a table just five feet away from two double beds. It was very unsettling to me.

"What brings you to the Singles Weekend?" he asked.

He put me at ease when he got up, turned on another light, and opened the curtains to look outside. My room looked out onto the pool, and there were people milling about right in front of the window having a "Midnight Splash Party." That was one of the activities scheduled for the weekend. I quickly forgot my fears.

"I came with Carol because she made it sound like a good way to get away from it all," I said.

"So, are you 'getting away from it all' in your room?"

"Well it was just too hot for me in the bar. I had to get out. I felt like an idiot fainting like that. How about you? What brings you here this weekend?"

He reached for a doughnut. Then he put the entire thing in his mouth at once.

I laughed, "Hungry?"

Powdered sugar fell down his chin. He was over six feet tall, but he looked three years old sitting there with his face and hands all dusty from the doughnut.

"Sorry, I never had dinner. Pete and I took off after work to get here on time and didn't stop. Those little hot dog things they had in the bar wouldn't fill a rat's tooth," he said with his mouth full, now spewing dust down the front of his shirt.

I went to the bathroom to get him a towel.

"Actually, I came along with Pete so I could get out of the house. I'm twenty-eight years old and I'm living with my parents again. Pretty pitiful, huh?" he asked, looking me straight in the eye.

I noticed his eyes were a mix of grey and pale green. They were very striking.

"Well, if that's pitiful, then I guess my life is, too. I haven't left home yet. I go to school full time, and only work part time in a supermarket," I said.

"School? How old are you?" he asked a little uneasy.

"Don't worry, it's college. Rutgers University. I'm a perfectly legal twenty-one, just last week as a matter of fact," I said a little too proudly.

"Well, happy birthday, then," he said.

I reached for my coffee. "What takes you back home again? Bad break at work?"

"No, I've been there for the past two years. My wife and I haven't gotten around to getting a divorce. I gave her the house because we have two kids, and it was easier for me to leave than it would be for her."

Deja vu. Until he said he was married, I had not thought of Carl. But when I did it was, strangely, not painful. I probably should have run for the door, but all of a sudden I felt a release. I was sitting across from a perfect stranger, and I felt good. It felt good. I finally had my life back. It was that obvious to me. I was having fun, and I was laughing. It was hard for me to believe, but I was actually happy.

The next night, the organized activities included tennis, another splash party, and a private party at the bar. I dressed more appropriately, so I would not faint from the heat. Carol and I entered the tennis match. I had never played tennis in my life, so it proved to be an interesting game.

Joe and Pete also entered the match, and when it came time for men against women, we wound up being opponents. I could hit the ball, but I couldn't get it over the net. Carol did all of the scoring. I just took up space. Joe was not much better than I was, so the game was really between Carol and Pete. Pete won.

We left there and went to the pool party. Pete still felt competitive and challenged us to a race. Carol could barely tread water, so she declined. Joe said that he wasn't interested either. I learned the previous night that he had been in the Navy and that he had only marginally passed the swim test requirement.

I, on the other hand, got cocky. I had been on the swim team as a kid and had many first place medals. Pete didn't know this, and I didn't volunteer it. I simply took him up on his challenge. The race was on. We had to do two laps of the Olympic-sized pool.

Carol said she would be the judge at the end, and Joe said he would be the starter. He went to the edge of the patio and picked up two metal trash can lids. He came back, yelled, "On your mark, get set," and then he smashed the two lids together to represent the starting pistol.

Pete and I took off. I was laughing as I entered the water because Joe looked so silly smashing the lids together. I didn't get enough air to start with, so I had to look up out of the water to breathe. I saw Pete, who one full body length ahead of me. So, I full throttled my strokes and kicked my legs like never before. I caught up with him at the end of the first lap, and I passed him on the turn. I finished the second lap a second or two ahead of him, and I was declared the winner.

Then we all decided that we'd go back to the bar. I drank ginger ale all night because I was still preoccupied with everyone knowing that I was not drunk the night before. Pete, Carol, and I danced some more. Joe said he didn't know how to dance, so he chose to hold up the bar like he did the night before.

A little later, Joe suggested that he and I go get some coffee and doughnuts and take them back to his room. I knew I could trust him, so off we went. We were only in the room for about five minutes when the phone rang. I was closer to it than Joe, so he said, "Will you get that?"

"Sure," I responded. Then I picked up the receiver. "Hello?"

"Hello, this is hotel security. Are you alone in the room with a man?"

"Yes," I said.

"Well, I would like to inform you that this is a respectable hotel. We do not appreciate such behavior in our establishment," the female voice said.

I started to stutter, "But we're not doing anything. We're just talking, really."

The woman on the other end started to laugh hysterically.

"Oh Maureen, you are so gullible. You're a typical dumb blonde."

I hadn't recognized Carol's voice until just then, and I really felt like an ass. My affair with Carl notwithstanding, I was still just a Catholic school girl who wanted to be perceived as doing the right thing.

Carol and Pete obviously got a great kick out of the practical joke. I could hear them both laughing. I gave the phone to Joe and told him what they had done. He invited them up to the room, and we all talked until five-thirty in the morning.

Then Pete came up with the idea to go watch the sunrise from the beach. We all trekked out to the sand. It was cold then, and the water did not look too inviting. Pete playfully challenged me to a race in the ocean. I told that him I wanted to go out a winner and I that wasn't about to go in the ocean. So we all sat down and waited.

The sun finally came up. It first peeked over the horizon, and then it quickly popped up to form a radiant orange ball. It was beautiful.

At that moment, Joe asked me if he could call me after we went home.

I gave him my phone number.

The weekend ended, and my life began again.

Chapter Six

On Monday, I cut class and slept. Staying up for about thirty-six hours had taken its toll on me, and I couldn't get up for school.

My parents didn't say anything about that. They knew I was twenty-one, paying my own tuition, and fairly responsible. So, Mom just let me sleep, and Dad just quietly suggested later that I not let it become a habit. I assured him it wouldn't.

Joe called me on Monday night. He asked me to go out the next Wednesday. I said yes. There was only one problem. He did not have a car. He left his only car with his wife and used public transportation to get around the city.

I told him I would pick him up. He gave me directions, and I drove into the city to get him. When I got there, he was ready and waiting for me outside. He climbed into the car very carefully. I was driving a brand new Volkswagen Beetle, my first new car, and I was very proud of it. However, it was not easy for Joe to get in or out of it. He was simply too tall. My five feet, two inches, fit just fine.

Joe and I went out to dinner in Philadelphia. I let him drive since I didn't know my way around very well. After dinner, we drove to a local club in New Jersey. We sat down at the bar. Joe knew the bartender, Bobby, and introduced me to him. I started to order my ginger ale when Joe said, "Come on, I know you weren't drunk that night, so you can order a real drink. Bobby, give her a gin and tonic."

I didn't bother to object, and I took a sip of my gin and tonic. I had never had gin before, and I found out that I didn't like the taste of it with the first sip. But not being too "bar-wise," I didn't know that when you push an empty glass away from you at a bar, the bartender refills it. Bobby was very quick to do just that. I figured that I would just drink it to be polite and get rid of it. Again, Bobby refilled it. Again, I was polite. I proceeded, on my first date with Joe, to politely get pie-eyed. I don't remember having any more drinks that night, but I don't remember the rest of the night either.

I found out later that Pete had come into the club, and I danced with him all night long. Joe didn't realize I was drunk, and he just sat at the bar while Pete and I danced. He began to think that I really preferred Pete to him, and he just figured he would finish off the date and call it quits.

When Joe finally caught on that I was drinking a lot, he asked Pete to follow us to my house, so I could have my car home and so he could have a ride back to the city.

On Thursday, I cut class again. This time, I was too hung over to get out of bed. Dad just bit his lip and hoped for the best. I'm sure he thought I was drinking because of depression, but I was actually having fun.

Joe called me on Thursday night to see if I was okay.

I asked him how I got home the night before. When he told me Pete drove him home from my house, I was shocked. I didn't even remember seeing Pete. I apologized for my behavior and admitted, "Yes, I was drunk, really."

"Maureen, are you perhaps, more interested in Pete than me? I mean, he likes to dance and so do you. I'd understand if you'd rather see him," Joe said, without taking a breath.

It took me a second to realize what he was suggesting. "No, God, no. I was drunk and I like to dance. But I really don't think I'd be interested in dating Pete. I'm sorry I behaved that way. I didn't mean to," I said, almost as quickly as he had.

Then I explained how I was trying to be polite.

He laughed, "Well, you pushed the glass away 'politely' at least five times."

Joe gave me a second chance and asked for another date.

Chapter Seven

It was April, and I was in my junior year of college. I was thankful that I didn't have too many more weeks of school left to finish the year, especially since I was tired from keeping such late hours.

Joe worked part time for his parents, tending the bar his mom and dad owned. They lived above the bar in a very nice, very large apartment. Since Joe would usually finish at midnight, I would leave my house at around eleven-thirty at night to pick him up so we could go out.

By the end of May, I had learned to get by on very little sleep. I would go to school between eleven A.M. and two P.M., do homework until four P.M., go to work from five P.M. to ten P.M., and pick Joe up at midnight to go out. I would get home anywhere from three A.M. to five A.M., and then I would start all over again.

Before my relationship with Joe became physical, I went to the doctor to get the pill. I feared pregnancy more than anything on earth. So when I saw that we were going in that direction, I told Joe that I had to be on the pill before I would even consider it. I had taken foolish chances with Carl by only using condoms as protection. One broke once, and I sweated for a month until I got my period, so I vowed that would not happen with Joe. He understood, and we waited until I was on the pill for a full month before we "did it."

Joe wanted to make our first time a special night, so when I picked him up, he had flowers and candy for me. We went out to dinner, and "I didn't get drunk." That became a joke between us, and I never drank alcohol on a date again.

After dinner, Joe drove to a Holiday Inn in Philadelphia. I began to feel uneasy about what other people thought of me again, so I asked Joe to check in alone, and I told him I would meet him at the side door. He said I was being silly, but he agreed. He knew how I felt about anybody knowing we were "doing it," stranger or not, so he checked in alone.

I drove around to the side door and parked the car. I waited at the door for Joe to let me in. It was locked from the inside. Needless to say, I was absolutely mortified when the door opened, and there stood Joe and the desk clerk together. The clerk had to unlock the door because it was their policy to lock all doors after midnight for their guests' protection.

The desk clerk was very polite. "Good evening, Ma'am."

I walked past him and mumbled, "Good evening."

When Joe and I got to the room, we shut the door and literally rolled on the bed laughing.

"Why in the world did you let that man come to the door with you?" I asked.

"I feel like I'm sneaking the Queen of England in for a 'quicky,' for God's sake," he said, between laughs. "When the clerk said he had to unlock the door, I was too embarrassed at that point to stop him."

I overcame my desk clerk phobia in the months that followed. Joe and I decided to call that Holiday Inn "home," and we ended almost all our dates by going "home" first. It was a good time in my life.

Chapter Eight

After a year of dating Joe, I was finally ready for graduation. I had cut down on the late hours and had gotten on a more manageable schedule. I didn't miss as many classes as I had at the end of my junior year. I no longer stayed out half the night, and Joe and I spent more time on the phone during the week, leaving weekends for dating.

Joe and I would go to the race track on Saturday mornings, where he'd bet rather heavily. He was a good handicapper though, because he almost always won. I would merely pick a horse because it was "pretty." He tried to teach me how to read a racing form, but I still went with my method. Sometimes it worked, but most times, it didn't. I would only bet five dollars, so I didn't lose that much. He, however, would bet one hundred dollars, which blew my mind, but I figured that it was his money, so I didn't care.

Joe decided to move to New Jersey and commute to work in Philadelphia by train. This made our time together more frequent. Three days before graduation, I picked him up at the train station after work as usual.

As Joe climbed into the car, he said, "I got you a graduation present."

"Oh, how nice," I said, "but you didn't have to."

He handed me a small box.

I opened it quickly. Inside was a very beautiful, solitaire diamond ring. I looked over at him.

"Will you marry me?" he asked.

"Yes," I exclaimed without a second thought. I hugged him over the stick shift of the car, and I said, "We have to go to my house and tell my mother."

When we got there, Mom was in the kitchen preparing dinner. I offered to help. She must have known something was up because I never offered to help cook dinner when she was home, only when she worked late. I kept putting my left hand obtrusively in her line of vision. She finally caught on.

"What's that on your finger?" she asked.

"Isn't it nice? Joe gave it to me for graduation," I answered.

"A diamond?" she asked.

"Yup," I said, "we're going to get married."

She put the pot that she was holding down and gave me a hug. Then she looked away. "What will your father say?" she asked.

I knew she was referring to the fact that Joe was divorced and that we couldn't be married in the Church. "I hope he hugs me too," I responded.

Dad was not as pleased about my news as I would have liked. But after a few days, he relented and gave us his blessing. His sister, my Aunt Kate, had told him that if he didn't give his approval, that wouldn't necessarily change my mind. Better to swallow one's religious pride than lose a daughter forever, she advised him. Thank God for Aunt Kate.

We planned an October wedding. I told my parents that since we could only be married in a civil ceremony, I would keep it small and private. Dad surprised me and said,

31

"Since I gave your sisters away with a bang, then I'll do the same for you." I was happy that he had come around.

Joe and I decided on the twelfth of October. This date came from a joke he and Pete used to have. They both said they would only remarry on the "Twelfth of Never."

But it was not to be. After starting to make arrangements for a hall and caterer, Joe's mother announced that she would not close the bar for our wedding. She insisted that we move the day to a Sunday. I thought Joe would stand up to her, but he didn't. And so, on Sunday, October 13th, 1974, Joe and I were married.

Chapter Nine

Getting married on the thirteenth would have set off alarms with a superstitious person. Neither Joe nor I were; perhaps we should have been.

On our wedding day, I got my period — so much for the passion of a wedding night. So, when we got to our hotel after the reception, we sat on the bed and opened cards to see how much loot was in them. We had gotten over $1000. That was quite a bit in 1974 for a couple who were starting out with very little.

The next morning, we left for our honeymoon cruise. We flew to Miami and boarded the ship to sail to St. Thomas, Nassau, and San Juan.

Little did I know that when a cruise ship leaves port, the casino opens. Joe found that out right away. He went to the casino and proceeded to lose all of the money we had amassed from the wedding. He didn't bother to tell me this, and it never occurred to me to ask how much he'd lost because he had said, "I only lost a little," when he came back to the stateroom.

Since all expenses are taken care of on a cruise ship, there was no need for me to notice that we had no money. However, when we reached San Juan, Joe and I got off the ship and went shopping. I immediately took a liking to an emerald pinky ring I saw in the window of a small store. We went in to look closer.

Joe said, "Why don't you just write a check for it, and we'll save our cash."

I laughed, "Now that's really stupid. We have over a thousand dollars. Why would I write a check?"

He sheepishly said, "I lost all the money on the first night. You'll have to write a check if you want the ring."

I was livid, and we left the store without the ring. Once we got on the street, I started to cry. I wasn't hurt, but I was furious. Tears were streaming from my eyes because I felt completely frustrated, and I could do nothing about the situation. I said, through clenched teeth, "You lost all of our money on the first night, and you wait until we're in a store to tell me? How could you?"

The signs of a problem marriage showed themselves right away, but I refused to think that his habit would become a problem. When we docked a week later and flew home, all we had for cab fare from the airport was the fifteen dollars I had in my wallet.

Chapter Ten

Joe and I got back into the swing of things once we got home. He went to work every day on the train, and I went to work at the supermarket.

I started to send out resumes so I could find a job using my degree. I had majored in English and minored in Journalism. I wanted to work in a publishing house doing editing work. However, there weren't many publishing houses in Philadelphia, and I applied to only one. When I returned from that interview, I told Joe I didn't get the job. I was very disappointed.

He said, "I hoped you wouldn't get the job anyway."

"Why?" I asked.

"Because if you did, you might meet someone better than me and want to leave me," he responded.

I couldn't believe my ears. I hadn't seen the insecure side of Joe in a year and a half of dating. But when it came through, it was gangbusters.

I decided that since I was making excellent money at the supermarket, and since Joe felt threatened, I would stay there a bit longer, until he could see that I wanted no one else but him. I cashiered for four more years.

During those early years Joe and I had good times. We were able to go away for the weekend without a moment's notice. Sometimes, we would just pick up and go to the mountains for a getaway. We also joined a bowling league and met some people who turned out to be life-long friends. We enjoyed our youth.

However, the gambling bug bit our marriage to pieces. We bought a second car so Joe could drive into the city and not have to wait for train schedules. We had a bank loan on that car, and Joe told me that he would make the payments through his checking account. When he didn't pay it one month, I wrote the check out of his account and gave it to Joe to mail. A few weeks later, the bank called to tell me that they hadn't received the last three payments on the car. I knew I had made them, and I pulled out Joe's checkbook to tell the loan officer the check numbers and the dates paid.

He said, "Mrs. Walker, we haven't received any of them. I suggest you call your bank and find out if those check numbers were cashed."

I called Joe's bank, and I was told that the account had been dormant for the past five months. No deposits or withdrawals had been made, and no checks had been written.

I was shocked. I couldn't believe Joe was so deceitful. I had about three hours to mull that over before Joe came home that day. I kept hoping that there was a better explanation than what I logically came up with. There wasn't.

Joe came in at seven o'clock, as usual.

I asked him how his day went.

He said, "Okay."

Then I said, "I had to call your bank today because the car payments aren't being paid."

He looked as guilty as sin. He reached into his pocket and pulled out a wad of fifty dollar bills. He gave them to me.

I counted it to be three thousand dollars.

"I went to the track today and won big. Pay the car payments that are due," he said with very little remorse.

I demanded, "What have you been doing with the paychecks that were supposed to be going into your checking account?"

Without waiting for an answer, I asked, "And did you plan on telling me you've been going to the track and winning? Or did you think you could pull this off without me finding out?"

He said, "I knew I was in trouble with the car payments, but I figured that one good win would pull me out of it. Today I had that win. I was going to tell you tonight. The bank just beat me to it."

I didn't believe him. I knew in my heart that if he had three thousand dollars in his pocket, he would try to make six thousand out of it . So I told him, "From now on, I'll pay all the bills through my checking account, and I will have control over all finances."

He agreed. He knew his weakness.

The years passed slowly, and Joe would have his slip-ups, but he would always tell me when he was in trouble. We began to use the term, "something stupid," to mean he was gambling and losing again.

It seemed like every year just before Christmas rolled around, Joe would do "something stupid." I began to recognize the symptoms. He would withdraw from me and start to pick fights with me over nothing. It would usually take a few days of badgering on my part before he would admit to "something stupid," but he would eventually have to tell me because the money was not where it was supposed to be.

One year, just after Thanksgiving, I saw the signs. I asked him about our finances. He told me that he had signed my name to loan papers and that the payments would come due any day. That year, we had seventy-four dollars to spend on Christmas, and we got that out of a change bank we kept in our closet.

But believe it or not, I still had faith that Joe would stop this behavior. After each slip, he promised that it was the last time and that he had learned his lesson. I chose to believe that, even though I knew it was very unlikely. I was disappointed many times.

Chapter Eleven

I finally left the supermarket in 1978. I took a job in an insurance company claims office. I was working there for a year when Joe and I decided to open our own trucking business.

Joe and I started with one small account. We borrowed $2500 for working capital and set up our business. We did very well, and eventually, I left the insurance company to work full time at the trucking company, which we operate to this day out of my home.

Looking back on it now, that was one of the best periods in our marriage. We were our own bosses, and we could see that we had great potential. That was when we decided to start a family.

I had been on the pill for a number of years, and I thought that by going off of it, I would become pregnant immediately. I was wrong.

After months of trying, with no success, I began taking fertility drugs. I was frustrated and depressed. I thought I would never have children. There was one time my period was a month late, and I was elated, but then the pregnancy test turned up negative, and I was crushed.

Soon, Joe and I had given up hope of ever having a baby and decided to buy another car to "get on with life."

We felt that since we couldn't have kids, we might as well have things. We bought an Alfa Romeo Spider convertible, a two seater. And that did it. Medical Science be damned. I was pregnant one month after we bought a two seater car.

For the next nine months, I walked on air. I was so happy to be having a baby. I would even talk to my stomach several times a day. I used to snuggle up to Joe in bed so that when the baby kicked he could feel it on his back. It was another good time in our lives.

On December 14th, 1980, Eddie was born. Joe had been calling him "Fast Eddie" for the entire nine months of my pregnancy. We had decided that Joe would pick out the name for a boy and I would choose the name for a girl. Since I didn't mind the name, Edward, I requested that his middle name be Neil — after my favorite singer, Neil Diamond.

My sister, Retta, went into the delivery room with me. Joe didn't want to see the baby born — "Too messy," he said. Retta had gone to all my prenatal classes with me as my coach, so when she asked if she could come in, the doctor said okay. He had delivered her last child as well, so everybody was family.

Eddie weighed in at nine pounds five ounces. I had endured thirty-six hours of very hard labor. I was given oxygen because I was experiencing shock and the doctor feared for the baby still inside me. When the baby's heart monitor showed he was in distress, the doctor decided to force the delivery. My tail bone was broken during the delivery, because the doctor had to use forceps to pull the baby out. The baby immediately started to cry. He sounded like a cat meowing. I said something about his strange cry, but no one paid any attention to me. After all, I was just the mother.

Eddie was only two days old when I complained to the nurse that he wouldn't suck when I tried to nurse him. She dismissed me as a new mom who didn't know what she was doing. On the second feeding that day, I watched Eddie's eyes roll back into his head. He went limp in my arms and started to turn blue. I was sure he was dead. I got up out of my bed and raced down the hall to the neonatal unit with Eddie in my arms. I knocked on the door and yelled, "There's something wrong with my baby."

A nurse came up to me and took Eddie in her arms. She looked down at him and said, "What's the problem?"

I couldn't believe it. He was alert and pink, and I was extremely distressed.

I yelled, "He turned blue and blobbed out," — this, from an English major.

She looked concerned and said, "We'll keep him in here and check him over. Don't worry. He'll be fine. You can go back to your room. We'll call you down if we need you."

I walked back to my room totally confused. I knew what I had seen. I prayed to God not to take him from me. I sat in my room staring at the clock, waiting for someone to tell me something. Finally, a nurse came in to tell me that they thought he might have pneumonia because an X-ray showed a spot on his lung. I felt relieved. Pneumonia is curable — no problem.

I called Joe to come to the hospital so we could worry together. I didn't want to be alone, but I refused to answer the phone. People were calling with good wishes, and I knew I would blurt out that something was wrong with the baby and hang up on them. So I stopped answering the phone.

After what seemed like an eternity, the doctor came in and told us that Eddie's heart rate was very slow. They didn't know what this indicated, so a Cat Scan was ordered.

I asked about the pneumonia.

The doctor said, "What pneumonia? Who said he had pneumonia?"

I said, "A nurse came in and told me that about six hours ago."

"Your child does not have pneumonia. I'll find out what's going on," he said.

When he left, Joe and I were extremely upset. Although Joe and I both pooh-poohed our Catholic faith to get married outside of the Church, our religion kicked in then. We agreed that the baby should be baptized as soon as possible, in case this hospital was going to kill him. We called the hospital chaplain to the neonatal unit, and he baptized Eddie right away. We felt that if they screwed up, at least the baby would go to Heaven.

The nurses would not let me feed Eddie because they had to monitor his intake. I used a breast pump, hoping they would at least give him my milk. But due to the immense stress I was under, I could not produce any milk. My milk had dried up in only three days.

Eddie showed no more symptoms like I described earlier until I was once again holding him to feed him. His eyes started to roll back into his head. I called the nurse. She finished with the premature baby she was tending and came over to me, but by the time she got to me, Eddie was fine again. The episode had only lasted about thirty seconds. I began to wonder if they thought I was nuts because they never witnessed what I said was happening.

It was an insane situation. By then, Eddie was four days old. I was forced to be released from the hospital because my insurance would not pay for me to stay any longer. I was healthy, even if my baby was not. So I commuted to the hospital every four hours to feed him.

On Eddie's fifth day of life, when he was once again in my arms, his head fell limp, and he started to turn blue. I screamed, "Now! He's doing it now! Please come look!"

A very quiet voice behind me calmly said, "I see it, Maureen. Don't worry."

A doctor had been standing behind me the whole time, and I hadn't even seen her there. I was so thankful, though, that she was there at that time.

The Cat Scan showed that Eddie had hemorrhaged in between the lobes of his brain. Blood was present, but they couldn't tell where it had come from. They told me that the blood would dissipate with time and that all we could really do was wait to see what might have been affected. The seizures would be treated, in the meantime, with Phenobarbital.

The doctor finally told us that we could take our baby home on Christmas Eve. I was ecstatic. What a Christmas present.

I read up on all brain injuries I could get my hands on in the next few months. I learned that one of the first symptoms of brain trauma in a newborn was a "catlike cry" and "refusal to suck properly while feeding." How dare they have ignored me? I may have been a new mother, but even in my ignorance, I was reporting classic brain trauma symptoms to them and I can't believe no one had listened.

It wasn't until Eddie was a year old that I was told he had "mild cerebral palsy."

"What do you mean, mild cerebral palsy?" I asked. "How is any cerebral palsy mild? And why did you wait until now to tell me this?"

The doctor understood my concern, in more ways than one. I was then seven months pregnant with my next child, and no one had told me anything about cerebral palsy. Joe and I had figured that since it took fertility drugs to conceive Eddie, I was still infertile. So, when I turned up pregnant when Eddie was just five months old, Joe and I took the news as a mixed blessing. It may have been sooner than we expected, but another baby was another miracle to us. And then, they tell us about the cerebral palsy.

I had two more months of pregnancy to sweat out, fearing that I would give birth to another child with cerebral palsy. I must say, though, that Eddie seemed to be developing normally. He even walked and talked at ten months. I questioned the fact that he had cerebral palsy. He never did have another seizure after coming home from the hospital. I had just assumed that the medication was working.

Chapter Twelve

Because of the stressful delivery of my first baby and the damage done to my cervix, I went into labor with the second baby at eight months. The neonatal unit was notified that I was considered a high risk delivery, so they had room put aside for my new baby.

Katie was born on January 27, 1982. She was shriveled up, deep red, and had no eyelashes, but she was beautiful and healthy. She was my little girl, and I was happy.

With Eddie, I had an easy pregnancy and a horrible delivery.

With Katie, I had a horrible pregnancy and an incredibly easy delivery. I attributed the tough pregnancy to the stress I felt worrying over Eddie's health and to the fact that Joe was not around very much because he was working. I had to spend a good deal of time in bed in the early months due to bleeding and the threat of a possible miscarriage. So, when all went well in the end, I figured that our lives would get on track again.

Our business was growing, as was our family, so Joe and I spent less and less "quality time" together. I knew he had to entertain clients with lunches and dinners, so I became a part-time secretary and full-time "house frau."

This turned out to be the beginning of the end of our marriage.

Katie was only three weeks old when I received a phone call from a woman who wanted to speak to Joe. I asked her for her name and what company she was with before I gave the phone to him.

She said coldly, "It's personal."

I gave Joe the phone.

He said, "No, I told you I don't want any." Then he hung up the phone.

It rang again almost immediately.

He answered, "I told you, I don't want any. Now stop calling here" he screamed into the phone. Then he hung up again.

The phone rang a third time.

By this time I was beginning to get suspicious. I said, "I'll answer it this time. Hello?"

The woman said, "Maureen, you don't know me. My name is Jane. Your husband and I have been having a relationship for the past eight months. He broke up with me today, and I thought you should know this."

I thought I was in a movie. Everything started moving in slow motion.

I don't know why, but I asked, "Why do you think I should know this?"

"Because", she said, "your daughter is named after me. Joe said it was his way of proving his love to me. That's why."

Chapter Thirteen

Now, one might wonder how my beautiful baby girl, Katie, could be named after someone named Jane. Here's how.

When Katie was on the way, Joe and I agreed she would be called Katherine if she was a girl. I could not find a name I liked enough to go along with Katherine, so when I filled out her birth certificate application, I left the middle name blank.

Joe came to the hospital that day, and when I told him I turned the application in with no middle name, he convinced me that Jane would be a good middle name for her. I fought him on that a bit because I really didn't like the idea of my little girl having the same name as two of King Henry VIII's wives. Katherine Jane sounded a bit pretentious to me, but I relented because he seemed so intent on the combination. He even reminded me that I had chosen Eddie's middle name. So, Katie came home from the hospital as Katherine Jane.

The bitch was right, I thought. He did name my baby after her.

My phone conversation with Jane lasted a few minutes longer. I don't remember it well, because, like I said, I was in a slow motion movie, and all I saw was Joe, standing in front of me and looking sick.

When I hung up the phone, I followed Joe up to the bedroom.

He started to get dressed to go out.

I said, "Oh, no, not this time, pal. I'm the one who's leaving. You stay here with the babies. I have to get away from you."

I got dressed and left the house. I didn't know where I was going to go. I only knew I had to get away from him. I drove around for a while, trying to sift through what I had just heard.

This phone call came when Katie was only three weeks old, and I was already in the midst of post partum depression. I had often found myself standing at the kitchen sink crying for no reason. She cried all of the time and, even if she was dry and fed, I couldn't make her happy. I've always argued that my mother wished this on me as pay back for my first two months of constant crying.

And, because Eddie was only a year old, I never seemed to have a moment's peace. When one baby napped, the other was up. I just wasn't getting enough sleep.

Now add to this depression, the news that my husband has been playing around for the past eight months. I was in a major blue funk.

After about an hour of driving in circles, I finally found myself knocking on my sister Nancy's door. I finally realized I needed to talk to someone.

I told Nancy about the phone conversation. She seemed just as shocked as I was. And then I decided I needed to know more. I called Joe at home to remind him that Katie was due for an eleven P.M. feeding and to ask him for

Jane's phone number. I said, "You might as well tell me the number because I'll find it out sooner or later anyway."

He gave me the number.

I called her and told her that I was no longer at home, so I could talk freely, without Joe listening to my every word.

She was surprisingly forthcoming. In a conversation that lasted for about forty minutes, she proceeded to tell me a wealth of disgusting information about my husband. I was to find out later, from Joe, that they had been out drinking all day, and she did seem drunk when she was so eager to fill me in.

I learned from Jane that she had met Joe at a bar. They had started dating around the time that I was bedridden with the threat of miscarriage. He was able to carry on with her because I believed that he was having business lunches and dinners with clients. Indeed, I was even paying the bills for these excursions because he was charging them on the company credit card.

Jane told me how often they would go to the shore for the day and spend the whole time in a motel. She mentioned that she had given my Katie all the embroidered sleepers and blankets that Joe had passed off as gifts from clients and contacts. Fool that I was, I wrote thank you notes to all of those people and never thought it odd that Joe insisted he hand deliver them.

Jane clearly wanted to hurt Joe by giving me all of this information. She didn't seem to care if she was hurting me in the process. She even told me that Joe would bring Eddie over to her house on Saturday mornings when I thought he was taking Eddie to see his mother.

Might as well have been. Jane was forty-eight years old to Joe's thirty-seven and my twenty-nine.

She said he especially enjoyed their rides to the shore because she would give him blow jobs in the car on the way.

So romantic, I thought.

The kicker came when she told me that she had been in my house. I couldn't fathom how that could have occurred until she elaborated further. While I was in the hospital giving birth to Katie, Joe brought her home with him. My sister, Retta, had Eddie for my stay in the hospital, and this left Joe free to do as he pleased. Jane and Joe played house for the three days I was gone. She cooked for him on my stove, made love to him in my bed, and even cleaned up the place so I would have a nice house to come home to.

After hearing all of this, all I said was, "You didn't do a very good job. I had to vacuum when I got home." Great comeback, huh?

Jane also told me that she had given Joe the expensive leather jacket he had been wearing.

I thought he had bought it for himself.

Then she mentioned that she had picked out all of my Christmas presents two months earlier. She even wrapped them for him.

Now, I ask you, *Who's the fool here?*

The damage had been done. I stayed at Nancy's for a few more hours, and then I went home to my loving husband.

Joe was sitting in front of the TV feeding our little girl her three A.M. bottle, when I got home. He looked absolutely ludicrous sitting there in his boxer shorts with the baby in his arms. He didn't seem to know what to do or say. Neither did I.

Katie was surprisingly cooperative. She went back to bed and fell right to sleep.

Then Joe and I went into our bedroom. He sat down on the edge of the bed. "I ended it with her today because I realized how much I really do love you," he said.

"Then buy me a new bed," I said. "I won't sleep in that bed ever again."

Chapter Fourteen

The next day, Joe hurried out to buy a new bed. I insisted that he also buy new sheets. Since I didn't remember which sheets were on the bed during their little tryst, I refused to sleep on any of our sets. I also rearranged all the furniture in the entire house. I felt that Jane had violated my home. I wanted everything in it to look differently than when she had been there. I would have been happier if I could have moved out altogether, but rearranging it was the best I could do.

While Joe was out getting the new bed, I was off to the Bureau of Vital Statistics. I had to change my baby's name. I still couldn't think of a name that went well with Katherine, but it was not going to stay Jane. I was so angry with Joe, I could taste it. I decided to give Katie my maiden name, Gavin, as a middle name. I didn't ask Joe's opinion. I brought home a form, threw it down in front of him, and said, "Sign it."

He did, with no questions or objections.

I had changed Katie's name just in time. She hadn't been baptized, yet. When she was, it was as Katherine Gavin. Her birth certificate was changed to reflect the new name. I sent Jane a copy to let her know that she didn't have the last laugh.

In the months that followed, I became a radical bitch. I ran hot and cold where Joe was concerned. I could not get Jane out of my mind. Every time Joe went out, I thought he was going out to see her. I started to drive by her house at all hours of the day or night when Joe was not home to see if he was there. He never was, but I couldn't stop thinking he would be.

One night, when Joe was late coming home, I became a raving lunatic. I called all over to find him. When I couldn't, I took his leather jacket out of the closet and slashed it to pieces with a carving knife. I wished he had been in it.

When he came home and saw the jacket, he reached out to hold me. He said, "Don't you realize I love you, and only you? I screwed up royally, and I can only ask that you forgive me. What else can I do? Tell me, and I'll do it. I love you too much to watch you go through this agony."

"Yeah, and you lost a good coat, too," I said sarcastically.

Chapter Fifteen

For the next few weeks, I tried to behave like a normal person. I was so confused. I didn't know if Joe loved me or even if I loved him anymore. I put myself on a major guilt trip. I thought God was punishing me at last for the damage I had done to Rita and her family during my time with Carl. I finally knew what it was like to be on the other side of the fence, and it was not pretty.

So, I started to go back to Church on a regular basis. I asked God to forgive me for my history. I begged Him to make sure that Carl's family had gotten over the grief our affair might have caused, and I hoped that Rita had gone on to some semblance of happiness. I hated knowing the amount of pain I had caused another human being. However, I took solace in the fact that I had not done to Rita what Jane had done to me.

On occasion, I would find myself disliking my own baby.

Illogically, I felt that since Joe had wanted her to be named after Jane, then she was Jane's baby. I obviously knew in my heart that this was not the case, but I couldn't help feeling like Joe wanted Katie to be Jane's child. These were the kind of demons I inflicted upon myself for months.

I finally sought help through counseling. I joined a group therapy session. This helped a bit because I realized that other people's problems were far more serious than a cheating husband.

One woman had lost two children in a house fire. Her baby boy was only Eddie's age, and she would never hold him again. Her little girl was only three, and they found her under the bed after the fire was put out. This snapped me back to reality. I still had my babies, I still had my life, and I began to get back on track. My problems weren't so bad after all. I knew I had to grow up and put more effort into making my situation better.

First, I had to learn to trust Joe again. My phone calls to check up on him began to lessen, although I felt the need to look attractive at all times. No matter how long it took, my make up and hair were always perfect. I also made sure the kids and I were dressed nicely, so he would have no need to go elsewhere again.

Our sex life had never been bad. In fact, I was completely perplexed when I learned of the affair because Joe was the one who would have headaches or be too tired for sex. I rarely, if ever, said no. So when he cheated, I couldn't figure out why. He couldn't say he didn't get enough at home.

After the affair, I became a sex fiend. I reasoned that he wouldn't have the need or the strength to look. I was always after him to make love to me. And when he would, I often worried that he was thinking of Jane.

Maureen Gavin

Chapter Sixteen

The further we got away from the night of Jane's phone call, the more I ran hot and cold. My need to pressure Joe for sex all of the time began to subside. In its place came periods of bitchiness.

Joe never knew when he came home at night if I was going to be nice or nasty. I found fault with everything he did. When I would take the kids out for a walk, he would often watch as we left the yard. He told me years later that he found that very endearing, that he loved me the most during those moments he saw me with the children and that he realized what a fool he had been to risk losing us, in his words, "for a piece of ass."

Needless to say, I would ruin this loving moment for him when I returned to the house because, immediately upon entering the house, I would bitch that he never wanted to go with us. I'd say things like, "I guess you'd rather be out with your whore than with your children, huh?" So, I slowly made myself the most undesirable person to be around, in spite of my physical attempt at perfection.

Joe tried his best to make things up to me. Our business was doing extremely well, so finances were not a big concern anymore. He still gambled, but he usually didn't get into debt over it. He bought me diamonds for my birthday, diamonds for Christmas, and diamonds because he had a good day at the casino. Joe was trying in the only way he knew how — by spending money on me.

One weekend, we went down to Atlantic City. Joe didn't like me to watch him gamble; he said I was bad luck. Interestingly enough, before we were married, I was his good luck charm. But since my money was at stake too, I was bad luck.

Joe spent hours in the casino, while I took the kids to the pool. When we met in the room before dinner, he showed me that he had won $5000. He told that me he wanted me to go down to the gift shop to see a watch he wanted to buy me.

The watch cost exactly $5000 because its face was surrounded with full-cut diamonds. It was beautiful.

I said, "It's really nice, Joe, but five thousand dollars? I'd rather spend the money on something more realistic."

He looked disappointed. We left the store without it. Again, we were on different tracks.

Joe spent the entire next day and night in the casino. I was on the beach or at the pool with the kids, alone again. Right before dinner, Joe came into the room. He had both hands behind his back. He said, glowingly, "Pick a hand."

I said coldly, "Give me the watch."

He tossed the watch on the bed with his right hand. It was wrapped in a pretty box with a bow on it. Then, with his left hand, he threw down several packs of one hundred dollar bills. I looked at the pile, afraid to ask how much was there.

"Thirty thousand dollars," he shouted. "Can you believe it?"

I have to admit, I was impressed, but believe it or not, I wasn't happy. I knew that if he could win that much, he wouldn't stop there. I was right.

On our last day in Atlantic City, Joe said he just wanted to try one last time before we headed home. So he went into the casino while the kids and I killed time around the hotel. We had already checked out, so all we could do was mill around.

Eventually, Joe came out of the casino. Because I had the kids with me, I could not go in to find him. I had to wait for him to come out. When he did, he looked sullen. He said only, "Let's go."

As we walked toward the main exit, Joe told me to go out to the car and that he would meet us there in a few minutes. When he came through the electric doors, I saw that he had a large brown bag under his arm. He got into the driver's seat and handed me the bag. "Open it after we pull out of here," he said.

I opened the bag. Much to my surprise, there was even more money in it than I had seen the night before, $43,000, to be exact. I couldn't believe my eyes.

Chapter Seventeen

On the ride home, we were like kids in a candy store. We talked about how we could spend the money. We decided to put an addition onto the house. We would add a garage and build a proper office. Thus far, we had been using a spare bedroom as our office, and the space was a bit cramped.

So, we called a contractor the next week. When we discovered that the addition didn't even put a dent in his winnings, we went whole hog and decided to redo the entire inside of the house. This meant ripping out walls, new bathrooms from top to bottom, new siding, and even landscaping the entire front and back yards. I finally got to change the house that Jane was in. Nothing remained the same except for our address.

As you might guess, this type of project takes many months to complete. The contractor wanted one third of the cost up front. No problem — we had $43,000. So, we gave the contractor $15,000, and the work began. After two months, he wanted another third. Joe only gave him $10,000 that time. I thought nothing of it. We still had plenty, and the contractor was happy with that. When the job was complete, the contractor gave me the final bill. I showed it to Joe when he came home that night. It didn't go well.

"Go to the bank, and get a cash advance on your credit card. We don't have the money," he said matter-of-factly.

"You didn't," was all I could think to say.

"Just do it," he said angrily.

Usually, after a big loss, Joe was like a little boy begging for forgiveness. This time, he was mad. That wasn't like him. I should have seen it coming, when he told me to short pay the second installment by $5000.

I went to the bank and got the rest of the money for the contractor. Then I owed the credit card company — at eighteen percent interest.

A month later, Joe came clean. The reason for his anger was the extent of his loss. He had signed markers at the casino in excess of $25,000 more than the $18,000 which was left of the original winnings. Once a gambler, always a gambler. We had a totally revamped house, but we also had a totally revamped financial standing. We met the payments, but life became strained, both monetarily and emotionally.

Chapter Eighteen

I began to refer to time as "life before Jane" and "life after Jane." We had certainly had our share of problems with Joe's gambling before Jane, but life after Jane slowly became intolerable.

Joe and I literally drifted apart. He started going out with golf buddies more and more and I joined bowling leagues without him. We rarely did anything together, and neither of us really minded it. Lovemaking dwindled, and I didn't care. I didn't even think about Jane, or any other women for that matter. He had his life, and I had mine. We co-existed. I had become very cold hearted, mean and sarcastic where Joe was concerned. I was always waiting for the other shoe to fall. I knew it was just a matter of time, and so did Joe. Neither of us spoke about it; we just knew it was there between us, like a big, ugly monster.

So, three years after Jane, Joe and I separated. It was February, 1985. Eddie was only four years old, and Katie was three. We didn't part well.

When Joe moved out of our house, he moved into the home of a woman I had not, at the time, known was in the picture. I found out about her quite by accident.

When he left, he gave me an address in Philadelphia. I never checked it out. When I mentioned to my girlfriend,

Marie, that Joe lived on Ritner Street, she said, "No kidding. I work on that street. What number is he at?"

"1224," I said.

She laughed. "Maureen, the hospital I work at is number 1224. No one lives there and there are no private homes on that block."

I had no trouble believing this. Joe always lied about stupid details. I figured this was just another bit of information he wanted to hide from me.

So, I hired a private investigator to find out Joe's true address. He hadn't even left the state. He was living with a woman just three towns away. Her name was Bess. The P.I. had given me Bess's phone number, too, but I continued to use his pager to reach him. I kept the phone number for future reference, but never told Joe that I knew where he was and who he was with.

I sought a divorce. Joe was hell-bent on fighting me at every turn. The only issue we agreed on was that I would keep the children with me, but I insisted that Joe see them at least once a week, so they would not become estranged.

I had watched, years earlier, as Joe walked away from his first two children because he hated his ex-wife. When she told him in anger that he could not see them again, he never looked back. He never fought for them. The last time we saw them, Jeff was seven years old and Lynn was six. So, nine years later, I was not going to let that happen to my children. I told him, "No matter what happens between us, do not leave these babies."

He didn't.

That was where our agreement ended.

Joe and I both retained lawyers, he went on the attack. He wanted to keep ninety percent of the business, and he was willing to give me the house, but he wanted half of everything in it, including my jewelry. He also went ballistic over my financial statement when he saw that I included twenty-five dollars per month for lawn care.

"Don't divorce me, and I'll leave everything as it is. You and I can both work the business and keep everything status quo," he said.

I couldn't figure out why he wanted to stay married. To this day, it still eludes me. But if all I had to do was drop the divorce in order for the fighting to cease, I gladly did so. After a year and a half of bickering and countless dollars spent on both sides for lawyers, I dropped the divorce.

That was 1986. The relationship Joe and I shared was strained at the very best. At worst, it was still combative. We'd argue over business decisions, and he'd come to the office in my house with a chip on his shoulder. We still couldn't get along well.

I attempted to keep the bickering to a minimum around the kids. Katie was still too young to comprehend the whole situation, but Eddie felt the impact. He would ask me when Joe was coming home and he would stand at the door on Sundays and wait to see him drive down the street. It nearly broke my heart.

"Do you still love Daddy?" he asked me one time.

I answered, lying through my teeth "Yes, honey, I do. But Daddy and I can't play well together, so we can't play at all."

Chapter Nineteen

In the first year we were separated, I started to date again. What an experience. I was scared out of my mind. I joined a singles club because all of my friends were married, and I was the odd man out. They always wanted to include me in their plans, but I was uncomfortable when it came time to pay the check and all the guys huddled together. I'd lean in and ask what my share was. They would be generous and say, "Don't worry about it," making me feel like a freeloader. So, I very briefly left the cocoon that was our friendship.

The club I joined had activities for both adults and children. I looked forward to the family activities for a dual purpose. The kids got to do many things I would not have thought to do with them on a regular basis. We'd have "Eat Out Nites" with other families, go to shows or the circus as a group, and have "Unbirthday Parties" for the little ones. They had fun, and I was meeting people, men and women included, who had something in common with me. I was no longer uncomfortable when the check came. We all split it evenly, and no one was odd man out. I made lifelong friends in this organization.

Everyone had "first date horror stories" to tell when we'd meet each other at either family or adult functions. It made life easier knowing that I wasn't alone in this endeavor, no matter how lonely I felt.

On one particularly lonely afternoon, I was feeling down about being thirty-three years old and no longer in "the white picket fence" mode. I had lost my dream of "happily ever after" and only had "ever after" to go on.

So, what better than go see a psychic? I had never believed in psychics before, and wasn't sure that I did then, but I felt the urge to speak to one. I gathered up the kids, and off we went.

The lady read the cards I drew out of the deck. She told me I had a very sad life.

Great. Just what I needed to hear, I thought.

But she wasn't speaking in the present tense. She said that my life had been sad and that this was about to change.

She he had my attention, saying that I would meet the man I would marry in two days, two weeks, two months, or possibly in February, the second month of the New Year. His name would begin with the letter D, G, or S.

I thought, "*Marry? Who wants to get married again? I'm not even out of my first marriage yet.*"

Then she startled me with, "You have psychic powers, my dear. You just haven't tapped them yet. You will find a need to do that soon. You will also have another child, a girl, with blond hair and blue eyes."

I was hoping that was bull because I wanted another kid like I wanted the plague.

She went on to tell me other things that afternoon, but the new man, the new baby, and the psychic powers were all I could handle. I paid her fee, gathered Eddie and Katie up once again, and went home.

I thought about these things intently for some time. Then I remembered that my fifteenth high school class reunion was going to be in two days. The prospects scared the hell out of me. But they gave me an uplifting feeling at the same time.

Chapter Twenty

The reunion came the following Saturday night. My girlfriend, Jill, and I planned to go together. She drove to my house, and we left from there.

Upon entering the room, I had forgotten all about the psychic. I got caught up in strolling down memory lane with all of my old friends. I was having a great time. No one was bothering to dance to the music because we were all so intent on conversation instead.

That's when I ran into David. He was tall, dark, and handsome. He joined our little clique and sat at the table with Jill and me. When he mentioned that he was recently divorced and that he had one daughter, I still didn't think much of it. But when he showed us a picture of his daughter, blonde and blue-eyed, I almost choked. The psychic hadn't said "a baby," she'd said "another child."

What I did next defies reason. I got up, left the table, and walked to the other end of the room. Basically, I panicked.

Jill came over to me some time later and said, "What happened to you? Why did you take off like that?"

I explained about the psychic.

Jill laughed. "Oh Maureen, you're so ridiculous. Come on back."

Maureen Gavin

I did, but I never spoke to David again — ever!

Chapter Twenty-One

I was so fearful of remarriage that I totally put the card reader out of my mind. I felt that since I had changed my fate by running away from David, none of the rest would come true either. So, I proceeded with my daily routine and took the kids to their nursery school classes. I went out on casual dates to the movies or bowling, and I enjoyed the tiny social life I had begun to etch out for myself.

My friend, Tommy, from the club, had come by often for coffee, and we would sit and talk for hours at my kitchen table. He was dealing with the recent death of his fourteen year old son, Tony, who was hit by a car when he was crossing the street in front of his school. I'd gotten to know Tony very well. My kids liked going to activities when Tony was there because he was a big kid who, surprisingly, liked to play games with the little ones at club functions. Tony had a slight speech impediment which made him pronounce my name "Mauween." I had found that endearing.

Eddie, then five years old and Katie four, took Tony's death surprisingly well. I didn't dwell on the tragedy of it when I had to tell them about it. I stressed instead, that Tony didn't look before he crossed the street; and that we must all make sure that we always look both ways before crossing to be safe in the future. They accepted that.

One night while Tommy and I sat talking in my small kitchen, he told me that he thought I should knock out the wall between the kitchen and the dining room to make the two small rooms one.

"Not on your life," I said. "I lived through reconstruction once, thank you, and that was enough. And besides, I don't have the money or the time for such a project."

Tommy said, "My buddy, Ross, and I could do it for you in two days. How much inconvenience is that? All you have to do is buy the materials and pay us for our time."

He made it sound so easy. So I thought about it for a week, and then I called Tommy to give him the go ahead. He sent me into a local supply store to purchase the materials he and Ross would need to complete the job. The fellow at the counter, George, was also a member of the same club, so Tommy had told him what I needed before I went into the store. He was very helpful. The following Tuesday night, Tommy, Ross, and George came over my house to dismantle my kitchen wall. I had expected Tommy and Ross, but George came too.

I had a pot of coffee on, and so I offered the guys some before they started to work. Only George took a cup; Tommy and Ross wanted to get going right away. George teased me that he was only there to supervise, and he sat at the table with me while the other two worked. All four of us talked while Tommy and Ross drilled, sawed, and generally made a mess of the wall. The whole first night was spent on destruction. Tommy promised me that the next night would be reconstruction.

When they left that night, my house was a shambles. Dry wall dust and nails were everywhere. I had to keep the kids away from the kitchen because I feared that they would step on something and get hurt.

But the next night, just like he promised, Tommy had finished the job and cleaned up all the mess. Then all four of us talked about why we joined the singles club. Tommy and Ross were both married twice, and George once. We all told our horror stories and talked about what we really wanted in marriage and in life in general. Obviously, we all wanted happiness, and we all felt it was out there, but we were having one hell of a time finding it.

"Since dating is still new to me," I said to them, "I'd like your opinion. Why is it, that I never get kissed good night on my first dates?" I asked.

"Really?" asked Ross, "If I took you out, I'd sure kiss you good night."

"I'll tell you why," said Tommy, with absolute self - assurance. "You give off the vibes that you're untouchable. I don't mean that in a bad way, just that you project a very ladylike manner, and that could put some guys off, at least as far as making the first move. They're waiting for you to tell them it's okay. I like to be in charge on my dates, and you'd make me think twice before kissing you, too."

"Gee, thanks," I said.

Tommy was very possessive, and he often lost out on relationships because he tended to smother the ladies he cared for; and he suffered from periodic bouts of depression over the loss of Tony. Ross was a bona fide pessimist. He felt that since he'd failed twice, he was doomed to be alone. But George was the most positive person among us. His only complaint was that the women had the better part of the deal. Women just had to accept a date, but the guy had to pay for it.

"I see women at the club all the time who have two or three dates in one week," George observed, "and I know that I can only afford one a week, with the cost of dinner and a show. Also, I like dating only one woman at a time, since every date has the possibility of being the real thing."

George was currently dating a lady name Claire, and he would often send her flowers for no reason other than to be nice.

I said, "You know, George, if you and I had been married to each other the first time, we would never have gotten divorced."

In all our conversations in the past two days, George and I had the most in common as far as wants go. We were both homebodies who wanted to spend time with our spouses, do nice things for them, and have nice things done for us. But Joe never thought of nice things like flowers, and George's wife didn't appreciate it when he did them. She had found the mailman more interesting than George. In fact, she married the mailman six months after their divorce became final.

Tommy, Ross, and George were planning a dinner party for the next night and spent a good deal of time talking about the menu they were preparing. I was surprised that all three of them cooked and baked. They were having quite a spread for their lady friends. Ross had a date for the night, and George had Claire. Tommy asked if I wanted to join them for the evening, even though he, too, had a date. I declined.

It was three weeks later when George came up to me at a Wednesday night dance and asked me if he could buy me a drink.

I accepted and reciprocated by buying him one as well.

"You know," he said, "it's funny. I sent Claire flowers at work this week, and tonight she broke up with me. She said I was getting too serious. Do you think flowers are too serious?"

I laughed. "Absolutely not. She's nuts."

He seemed a bit down, so I added, "Don't worry. There are plenty of women out there who'd appreciate a nice guy like you. Keep trying."

"You're a nice woman. Do you want to go out Friday night?"

"Yeah, that's it, just ask anybody. You're bound to get a yes with a line like that," I joked.

"It's not a line," he said seriously.

"Oh, I'm sorry. I thought you were being funny," I said.

"Sure, I'll go, but I have to see about a sitter before I can say for sure. Can you wait until tomorrow for a firm answer?"

"No problem," he said. "Can you give me your phone number?"

I did.

Chapter Twenty-Two

The next day, I called my nephew, Jack, to baby-sit. That way, I didn't have to worry about taking the kids out of bed to take a sitter home. That was one of the problems of being a single parent. I couldn't leave the kids asleep in bed alone while I transported the baby-sitter. There were several times I had to wake the kids up, put on their coats, and take them with us. Jack, could stay overnight, and I'd take him home the next day.

George called around six-thirty that night, and we made definite plans for Friday. He suggested we go to dinner and a show at a local comedy club. When he said he had to work until seven o'clock, I said, "Let's skip dinner and just go to the show." I remembered our conversation about the cost of dinner and a show, and felt that if we skipped dinner it would lighten his burden.

George arrived at about seven-thirty. He looked very nice in his three-piece suit. George stood about five feet, eight inches tall. He was bald on top and wore what could best be described as a handle of hair across the top of his head. He claimed, that way, when he looked in a mirror and saw hair, he felt less bald. Be that as it may, the hair he had, was light brown and wavy. His eyes were a beautiful blue. And, he had a charming smile.

I got my coat on and we left for the comedy club. We sat at a table and ordered drinks. We enjoyed conversation until the first comedian came on. After the show, George mentioned that he had not eaten dinner because he came straight from work, so he suggested that we go out to breakfast.

I felt really bad. I hadn't realized that by flippantly saying, "Let's skip dinner and go right to the show," the poor man wouldn't eat all day. So I said, "How about we go back to my house, and I'll make you breakfast instead?"

He agreed.

When we got back to my house, Jack was asleep on the sofa bed in the rec room. We quietly tiptoed past him and into the kitchen. I apologized again for the dinner mishap and proceeded to cook George some bacon and eggs. We talked for hours across the table. In no time, it was four-thirty A.M., and George decided that it was time for him to go. He stood slowly, walked around the table, put his hands on my shoulders, and kissed me, albeit tight lipped. He said, "Your record is broken. You've now been kissed on a first date!"

I laughed.

Then he left.

Chapter Twenty-Three

George asked me for a second date the next day, during a long phone conversation. It seemed we never ran out of things to talk about. His hours at work were long, so a good bit of our time was spent on the phone until the wee hours of the morning.

I knew he only dated one woman at a time, so it became clear that I was the one. I told him that I still intended to date others, since I had no set rule like that. He didn't object.

I continued to see others on casual dates, but I was rapidly becoming more and more attracted to George. In fact, he became uppermost in my thoughts after we had spent an evening at the skating rink with my kids and several other young ones from the club.

Eddie had fallen down on the rink floor and screamed bloody murder. I knew he was hurt, but I didn't realize how badly until he refused to stand back up on his skates. George skated over to him and gently picked him up. He skated off the floor holding Eddie. When he put him down, the protruding lump told us that his shin bone was broken and almost cutting through his skin.

I took off my skates, Eddie's, and Katie's too. I was going to drive Eddie to the hospital, which, luckily, was just down the street from the skating rink. George followed us in his car. He carried Eddie into the emergency room, while Katie and I tagged along behind them.

Once inside, I was ushered into an examination room with Eddie. George said he would stay in the waiting room with Katie until we found out what was going to happen. It took about three hours before we were told that Eddie would have to stay the night after they cast his leg. And George happily kept Katie amused the whole time in the waiting room.

I finally called my mother to pick up Katie when I realized that I would be staying the night in the hospital. George sat with her until Mom got there. She had not yet met George, so he introduced himself when Katie greeted Granny upon her arrival.

I came out of the cubical Eddie was in long enough to kiss Katie goodbye and explain to Mom what was happening. She seemed annoyed that a strange man was in charge of her little granddaughter for such a long period of time. I explained to her, as I walked her and Katie out to her car, that George and I had been dating for awhile and that he was very good with both of the children. She seemed to accept that and went home with Katie.

I went back inside to George, who had been patiently waiting for me to say goodbye to Mom. "Thank you for staying with Katie, George, I really appreciate it," I told him sincerely. Then I kissed him lightly on the cheek. He left me then to go get some coffee in the cafeteria.

George and I stayed at the hospital with Eddie the rest of the night, and as it turned out, I had to stay the next night too.

Chapter Twenty-Four

I had to call Joe from the hospital to tell him about Eddie's broken leg. Because it was an emergency, I decided not to page him, and finally made use of the information the private detective had given me a year before. I called Joe at Bess's house.

When Bess answered, I said only, "This is Maureen. Is Joe home?"

She audibly gulped and said, "Uh, no, he isn't. Can I take a message?"

I gave her the phone number to Eddie's bedside phone, and I said coldly, "Tell him to call that number when he gets in. I'm at the hospital with his son."

She asked, "What happened?"

I answered, "I'll speak to Joe when he calls, thank you."

Then I hung up. I didn't figure I owed her any explanation whatsoever. Disquieted, I walked down the hall to Eddie's room. When I got there, Eddie was on the phone. I was astounded. Joe had probably been standing next to Bess when she denied to me that he was home. When he had found out Eddie was in the hospital, he called the number immediately, before I could even reach the room.

I let Eddie explain what happened to him, and then I took the phone from him. Joe proceeded to blast me for taking four and five year old children roller skating. I ignored his tirade and told him what room Eddie was in. In about forty-five minutes, Joe came to the hospital to see Eddie.

After a brief visit, Joe kissed Eddie goodbye and told him he'd see him in the morning. Then we both left Eddie's side. We walked down the hall together, but he never questioned how I knew where, or who, he was living with. However, he did say, "You could have paged me. You didn't have to call there."

I responded, "I know. I just felt like talking to you, not a pager."

With that, we reached the elevator.

The doors opened, and there stood George, coffee in hand.

George chose to exit the elevator and not acknowledge me.

Joe said goodbye and stepped into the elevator car.

I laughed once the doors closed because it seemed like such a ludicrous situation.

Chapter Twenty-Five

Eddie came home from the hospital after a two day stay. I picked Katie up from my mother's, and we all went home together. Eddie was forced to walk on crutches and, being only five years old, he was not doing too well. He took to the stairs on his butt rather than trying to master the crutches. Poor thing. He looked so pitiful trying to maneuver around.

I decided I shouldn't go out while Eddie had trouble moving around, so George and I began to spend a good deal of time at my house. We were becoming close, and I looked forward to seeing him regularly. I, too, finally stopped dating others.

George and I decided to become intimate one night when an R rated movie on TV put us both in the mood. It was, however, four o'clock in the morning, and neither of us wanted to start something we might be too tired to finish. So, we agreed that he would come back on the following night. We planned to have a nice intimate dinner after the kids went to bed and start fresh.

The next night, all seemed to be going as scheduled until my girlfriend, Judy, stopped by to visit and brought along her boy, Craig. Eddie, Katie, and Craig were good buddies, and we always attended the same club functions together. So, enforcing a bed time when Craig was still there was impossible, and I couldn't very well tell Judy that she was interrupting the pending love fest George and I had arranged. George understood, and did nothing to encourage Judy to leave. Our romantic dinner was put on hold until almost ten o'clock, when Judy and Craig finally left.

After dinner, George and I had some champagne and relaxed by the fire. We snuggled up together there before we took the long trip up to the bedroom. I had not had sex for over a year, so to say I was nervous was an understatement. George was not one to bed everyone he dated, so he was apprehensive as well. Neither of us told the other this at the time though. We both tried to be cool about it.

The first time was great, although it was very fast. We both rushed everything. The second time, about an hour after, was stupendous. We took our time and made love like we meant it.

It took awhile for me to remember that George and I had our first date on February 28th, the second month of the new year. And his name fit the D, G, or S pattern that the psychic had predicted. This time, however, I didn't run to the furthest corner. I laughed when I told George about the prediction so he wouldn't take my observation as a proposal.

He said, "My daughter has blond hair and blue eyes. Maybe there's something to this."

Chapter Twenty-Six

George and I became "a couple" at the club. While it was a singles organization, they allowed what was called "unrecognized couples" to continue to attend. The reason for the rule was that, since the group was formed to promote meeting other singles, a newcomer should not have to be faced with a room full of couples.

So, once inside the door, you were expected to socialize with everyone and not take offense if someone asked your partner to dance. We were all there for a good time and to help others adjust to their newly single status.

George and I were both heavily involved in the club. We were on the Board of Directors, which ran the various adult and family functions. I attended both, while George kept his participation primarily adult-oriented. His two children lived with their mother, Billie, over an hour's drive away. So, I had not yet met them.

It seems I'm destined to meet and fall in love with men who have two children, a boy and a girl. If it ever be tallied, had I married all of these lovely men, I'd have six step-children.

I finally got to meet Chris and George III in April. George brought them to stay with him over Easter break. I suggested that they stay at my house while he went to work. It seemed silly to make them stay in his apartment alone for the entire day, so in the morning, he'd drop them off at my house on his way to work. Chris was thirteen, and George III was eleven. They got along well with Eddie and Katie, even though there was a difference in age. Chris liked to play with Katie and her Barbie dolls, and "Little," as George III became called, enjoyed being looked up to by Eddie. He was finally a big brother, instead of just Chris's little brother. The whole situation seemed to be working out.

But, as with all things in my life, the other shoe was about to drop.

Chapter Twenty-Seven

It was May 29th, 1986, when I got a message from Joe's sister, Lori, on my answering machine. I had not spoken to her since Joe and I had separated a year and a half earlier. There was no bad blood between us, just bad geography. She lived in Lancaster, Pennsylvania. I had not seen her since their mother's funeral, only two months before Joe and I parted. So, a phone call so suddenly seemed ominous. I returned the call as soon as I got the message. "Hi Lori, it's Maureen. What's the problem?" I asked.

She replied, "Hi, I'm really sorry it's taken me so long to get around to calling you. How are you doing?"

I knew she wasn't just interested in my welfare, but I went along anyway. "I'm fine, and how about you?" I asked.

"Well, I have a slight problem," she said. "I have Joe's daughter here with me. Do you know how I can reach him?"

"No. He's out of town. What happened?"

"Lynn ran away from home. I called her mom, but all she said was 'Go ahead and keep her. She's too much for me to handle.'"

"That's terrible." My heart went out to this child I had not seen in ten years.

"I don't know what to do," she said, sounding exasperated.

"I think Joe periodically checks his machine for messages."

"He better," she said, even more put out.

"Listen, just keep Lynn there until I can reach Joe, and then I'll get back to you."

I could not page Joe across the country, and I was not about to call Bess and fill her in on this new wrinkle. So, after some soul searching, I opted to call Lori back and tell her I would take Lynn off her hands. I told her, however, that I would have to talk to Lynn's mother and get some kind of documentation that proved I was allowed to take this minor into my home. I didn't want to be accused of kidnapping.

I drafted a semi-legal looking document, which stated that I was Lynn's step-mother and that I had the permission of her mother to provide a temporary home for her and seek any emergency medical care she may need while she was in my care. I had Lynn's mother sign this, and Lori, witnessed the signature. Then I brought this total stranger home to meet her half-brother and sister.

Lynn was a pretty girl, with blond hair and blue eyes. It was not George's daughter the psychic saw; it was Joe's. I was then responsible for raising another child, a sixteen year old problem child at that.

Chapter Twenty-Eight

George and I had been carrying on our relationship with very few problems. However, on Labor Day weekend, I could not reach him to tell him of the impending arrival of my "new baby." He was on a boating trip with his two kids and as unreachable as Joe was.

So, I explained the situation, as best I could, to the only two people who would feel the change immediately, Eddie and Katie. I started by telling them that before Daddy married Mommy, he had married another lady. "Daddy had two other children, Jeff and Lynn. Now, Lynn has problems with her mommy, and she's coming to live with us. She's your older sister," I finished.

"We have a sister besides Katie?" Eddie asked.

"Yes," I said, "and she needs our help."

"How long do we have to help her?" he asked.

"Until she doesn't need help anymore," was all I could think of saying.

So, off we went to Lancaster, Pennsylvania, to see our new family member. I left the kids with their cousins, while Lori and I set off to pick up Lynn's belongings at her mother's house. She explained that Lynn was not a bad child, but that she absolutely refused to cooperate with her new step-father. And Mom had chosen her new husband over her child. All she asked of me, even after hearing that Joe and I had not lived together for nearly a year and a half, was that I give her my phone number. She didn't mind that Lynn wasn't going to live with her father, as long as she didn't live with her.

I felt so bad for this poor girl. She had a bloody eye, which looked even worse because she had been crying all night.

Her eye was not black, but the eyeball itself was injured and red. I didn't ask, at that time, how it happened. We took her bag, and we left the only home she had known all her life.

We drove back to Lori's house in virtual silence. She was going home with a woman she hardly knew, and I was just as scared, only I didn't have the luxury of showing it.

When Lynn saw Eddie and Katie, her faced finally brightened up. She picked Katie up in her arms, "I finally have a little sister," she said. "I always hated being the baby. Now I'm not."

I thought this was a good sign.

Chapter Twenty-Nine

I still had to talk to the two men in my life about Lynn.

Joe finally called in after the holiday weekend was over. I gave him news about the business and then said bluntly, "I have your daughter here."

"What do you mean, my daughter?" he asked.

"Lynn," I said. "Her mother wanted her out of her house, and your sister wouldn't take her in."

"Oh shit, I'm still in North Carolina. I'll have to talk to you when I get back."

"Okay, talk to you later," I said. I hung up.

George called me from work on Monday morning. I broke the news to him. I told him we needed to have a serious talk, so he'd better stop by after work. I had supper ready for him when he came in. I introduced him to Lynn. She was polite and pleasant to him. Then she went down to the rec room with Eddie and Katie.

George and I had been having our private times after the kids went to bed. He was over often, but I always threw him out at around four-thirty A.M. so they wouldn't see him there in the morning. This would have to change with a teenager in the house. I broke it to him the best way I knew how.

"The little ones have no concept of sex," I faltered. "But a teenaged girl would certainly know what goes on behind closed doors. I can't have you sneaking out at four-thirty A.M. with Lynn here. We either cool this relationship now, or I have to ask you to commit yourself more fully and move in. This way, even though we're not married, she can see that we don't just screw around." I waited for his reply.

He said, "I have to go buy some lumber." He stood up from the kitchen table and grinned like the Cheshire Cat. "Well, your bed squeaks as it is now. Lynn will know what those squeaks are, so I'm going to buy lumber for a squeak-proof platform bed," he said.

I reached out to hug him. He was a sweetheart and I really loved him. So, the first night Lynn met George, she watched, perplexed, as he built a bed in our room.

Chapter Thirty

The first few months of our happy home were just that —happy. Lynn explained that the damage done to her eye was caused by a hit from her older step-brother, Joey. She said he beat her regularly, even though he was only five years older than she was. I asked why her mother tolerated this. She said that with her step-father's five kids, her, and Jeff, her mother was often overwhelmed, and that she would let a lot of things go unpunished. I told her that didn't happen in my house.

Once Joe had gotten back into town and heard the saga of how I inherited his daughter, his first knee jerk reaction was, "You're not getting any more support out of me for this."

I couldn't believe my ears. "I don't want anything from you. I just want to give your daughter a home," I screamed at him.

He backed down from his anger almost instantly. Not long after, he came over to meet his daughter for the first time in ten years. He haltingly stumbled upon first seeing her, "Your mother and I had some very serious problems that resulted in my not seeing you all these years. It's not that I don't love you and Jeff very much. I do. It's just

90

unfortunate that it turned out the way it did. Do you have any questions you'd like to ask me?"

"No," Lynn said, "I'm just happy to get to know you now."

It seemed we were off on the right foot for the time being. Joe would take Eddie, Katie, and Lynn out on Sundays. They would often go to Bess's house for dinner.

I wanted nothing to do with Bess since the bitch had interfered in my marriage. I may have had George in my life then, but I didn't have him when Joe and I were together, so Bess, who was around back then, was not welcome in my home when they would return from Sunday outings. Joe knew this, and he didn't push it.

It wasn't long after Lynn moved in with us that Joe and Bess had a falling out. It seems that she felt she should be raising Lynn. Joe wouldn't hear of it, and she accused him of wanting to leave her to go back to me.

How little Bess knew about me. I didn't want Joe back on any terms. But, I see it this way, Bess felt that since she took him from me, I might be trying to get him back by using his oldest daughter. What a fool. I already had two of Joe's children, and I didn't use them for any such purpose. There's no reason why I would start with Lynn.

The bottom line was that Joe came to know that I was not after any more support money, or anything else for that matter. He realized I was just, in his words, "a good person," and he was finally sorry for all the grief he had caused me over the years.

Joe and Bess broke up for good in July. I told him then that any lady he decided to take up with in the future was welcome in my house, that my children would respect them, as would I. This was the beginning of a friendship with my husband of twelve years.

Chapter Thirty-One

George and I introduced Lynn to Chris and Little. Chris and Lynn became fast friends. Chris liked Lynn because she got to do things at my house that her mom wouldn't let her do at home. Lynn was three years older than Chris, but we let them go to the mall to hang out. Chris was particularly happy that she no longer had to drag her obnoxious younger brother everywhere she went. Billie, Chris's mom, insisted that Chris take Little everywhere. And, as any thirteen year old girl knows, a brother makes a complete ass out of himself and you every chance he gets. So, Chris enjoyed coming to see her dad more and more.

One night, Chris and Lynn were in a creative mood. They were pretending to be hairdressers. They had played around with each other's hair for about an hour, when they seemed to exhaust all of their creativity. So Chris came up with the idea to do George's hair. "Dad, can we mousse you up?" she pleaded.

"What do you mean 'mousse me up?'" he asked, confused.

"You know, spray mousse on your hair, and style it."

"Go for it," he said with a grin.

So both girls sprayed him full of sticky mousse, and began rubbing his head like a Buddha's belly. After a few minutes, they had what little hair George had, sticking straight out sideways. His treasured handle of hair was at least three inches longer than the rest of it. He looked like a cross between Bozo the clown and a punk rocker. He loved every minute of it.

George and I had scheduled a trip to Disney World for August of that year, so I had to buy an extra ticket for Lynn. We arrived in Orlando with five kids in tow. Yours, mine, and ours was how George and I referred to our expanded family. Since Lynn didn't really belong to either of us, we opted to consider her ours.

We weren't in our apartment for more that two minutes when all five kids went scouting to see our home for the week. They all went ballistic when they saw the four person Jacuzzi in the master bathroom.

"Can we please take a bath?" squealed Katie.

"Sure, knock yourself out," I said.

Four of the five kids scrambled for the suitcases to find their bathing suits. They couldn't wait to get into the tub together. Lynn, however, went to sit quietly on the balcony.

I went out to see her. "What's up?" I asked.

She turned to look up at me. She had tears in her eyes. "I'm so happy and so sad at the same time," she said. "I've never been treated this well before, and I don't know why you're being so good to me."

"You're worth it," I said, "I'm not treating you any better than you should be treated." She sprung up and hugged me.

She had never touched me before, so I hadn't realized how tall she was. I had to reach up to put my arms around her. I held her for as long as she wanted. We cried together, against the noise of the other children splashing happily in the tub in the next room.

The week went by fast. Chris and Lynn spent most of the time off on their own. Little, a bit of a hyper kid, took off, too, on his own. I didn't like that, since he was only eleven years old, but George didn't mind since Little popped up every so often in the same lines we were in with Eddie and Katie. Plus, we always established meeting times and places so we could keep tabs on everybody's whereabouts. Nobody got lost or kidnapped, and George and I managed to get all five kids home safely every night.

Chapter Thirty-Two

September came around, and I enrolled Lynn, as a Junior, in our local high school. Normally, since I did not have legal custody of her, I could not have done this. It would have taken her biological mother or father to do so. However, since I had the same last name, I signed all of the necessary papers and no one bothered to ask me if she was really my child.

Lynn met some new friends at school, and soon, the house was bustling with teenagers. This was an experience I did not have time to grow into, like most parents, so I had to adjust quickly. I liked all of her friends, and they seemed to like me and George as well.

George and I established rules and curfews for Lynn, and she kept to them very well. On a very few occasions, she pushed the limit on the curfew, but she would always call to let me know why she was delayed. She was very responsible. I couldn't comprehend why her mother had so much trouble with her. I was having none.

I would often let Lynn baby-sit for Eddie and Katie when George and I would go out to the club on Sunday nights. I paid her as I would have any other sitter, so she had her own source of income in addition to allowance for chores. I had an additional phone line put into her room, so she would not tie up my business line with her friends. She was supposed to pay for any toll calls she made. That eventually became a sore point, however, since she started calling her old friends in Lancaster. The bills started to add up to almost one hundred dollars a month. And, since George and I didn't go out often enough to pay that in baby-sitting fees, she was in the red. She would then baby-sit for no pay and her phone bill was reduced by the amount I would have paid her, had she not owed me.

The situation, however, began to get out of hand when her total phone bill got to be over $400. She opted to get a job at the local mall, but she was in over her head and could not bring the balance down, especially since she continued to talk to Lancaster and run it back up again. I decided to just let the balance sit and "worry about it tomorrow." I paid the bills as they came due, and she owed me the money.

It was after she started working at the mall, in a candle and gift shop, that I noticed that she was beginning to accumulate an awful lot of store merchandise in her room. She said that she got an employee discount on everything and that she was decorating her room to her liking. Little did I know, she was getting the "five finger discount" by robbing the store blind whenever she was left to close up. It never occurred to me that she was stealing, since she so openly displayed everything.

At Christmas time, Lynn lavished the kids with extremely expensive presents. I had my doubts at the time about how she could afford them, but I chose to ignore it. I had no reason to think otherwise. I knew she worked a lot of hours, so I let it go.

The shit finally hit the fan when, several months later, I came home from shopping and there was a note on my door to call the local police department. When I checked my machine, there was also a phone message to call them as well.

I immediately called the number the police had left, and they told me Lynn was in the hospital. She had been caught shoplifting in Strawbridge & Clothier and she was found with more than $500 worth of clothes in a bag. When she was confronted, she faked a heart attack so convincingly that the store security called an ambulance and had her taken to the hospital. Imagine, a seventeen year old having a heart attack. She was good.

I called Joe and told him to meet me at the hospital. My suspicions were finally confirmed, and I told Joe what had been going on in my house. I don't know which of us was more angry.

A policeman was at the hospital waiting for us. He explained that we could take her home as soon as she was released from the hospital, but she had to go to the station because Strawbridges was going to press charges. The officer was very nice and suggested that we make it the next day since "she's been through a lot."

Joe and I agreed that she hadn't been through enough. We told the officer that we wanted to take her into the station right away. We wanted her to be fingerprinted and photographed like the criminal she was. We wanted to make her feel the humiliation of what she had done. We were both appalled that she felt the need to steal when we were both giving her more than she had ever had in her life. We were pissed to say the least.

Joe stood by any and all decisions I made regarding Lynn. He figured that since I was the one raising her, I had the final say in what happened to her. So, I took her in for counseling.

The counselor usually saw Lynn for fifty minutes, and then I would talk to him for the last ten minutes. He never violated her confidence, but he helped me understand why she did the things she did. Basically, she was crying out for her father's attention. Even though she said she wanted to have a friendship with him when she came to live with me, she was trying to punish Joe for all those lost years. She also resented having to share Joe with Eddie and Katie. She wanted him for herself.

Lynn bordered on incestuous when she wrote him a letter that said that she wanted to love him and have him love her and only her. She didn't like the little ones always being with her and Joe when they went out on Sundays, she began to mistreat Eddie and Katie when she baby-sat. I didn't discover this until a year later when they finally told me what had been going on when I left them in her care.

Chapter Thirty-Three

Lynn and I continued counseling for a year, but the situation didn't really improve. I would notice money missing from my wallet, but I would tell myself that I had just forgotten where I spent it. I didn't want to think that Lynn would steal from me. A store was one thing, but not me.

Lynn also jumped from one boyfriend to the next. In the beginning, she introduced me to them, but then she started running out the door when a car horn honked in front of the house. We were not getting along very well.

George and I came home early one night from the club to find her in bed with a boy I had never met. I walked in on her because I thought she had fallen asleep with the light on. When I opened the door to reach for the switch, I saw the young man's butt staring me in the face. I backed out of the room, and in a few minutes, they both came out fully dressed. The boy virtually flew out the front door, and I never saw him again.

I tried to put this behind me, but it soon became evident that the situation would have to change. One night, Lynn asked if she could stay overnight at her friend, Tracy's, house. All would have been well, had Tracy's mother, Carol, not called me that night looking for her daughter.

"I thought they were at your house," I said to Carol.

"No, Tracy said she was staying with you for the night."

"Well, if they get to your house first in the morning, give me a call, and I'll do likewise," I said.

Both girls were in for a heap of trouble for this one, and I had the honor of seeing them first thing in the morning. I told Tracy to go home and be ready for a blasting because her mom and I knew about their plot. She went home to face the music, and Lynn paced back and forth until I got to her.

I didn't bother to ask Lynn where she had been. By then, I really didn't care. I told her that since she was going to turn eighteen in the next month, she would be a legal adult. "I'm washing my hands of you. You can have a place to stay here, but you are on your own," I said bluntly. "That means that you do not need to lie about where you are going or who you are with. You don't have to tell me, and I won't ask. Along with that, however, I will not be your taxi cab to and from work or school. And when you graduate, you will pay rent to live here. As far as I'm concerned, you are a boarder in this house." I held nothing back in my anger, but I didn't expect what happened next.

Lynn looked at me as if I was dirt under her feet. Then she said, "Kiss my ass," and walked out the front door. That was May 29th, 1988. It had been two years, to the day, since I had taken Lynn into my home.

Lynn came back to the house only once to pick up her belongings. Tracy's mom, Carol, took Lynn in for the two weeks after she left here in a huff. I warned Carol to watch her money because of Lynn's history. Then I had packed Lynn's things in large trash bags, left them in my living room, and told her to come and get them.

What I found when I cleaned the room up astounded me. After the shoplifting incident, I thought I knew how much she had taken from her employer. I was really surprised when I opened her closet to find, easily, over $4000 worth of brass statues, dolls, candles, and porcelain figurines. All I wanted to do then was get all of this stolen merchandise out of my house as soon as possible.

The clincher came when I found a box filled with letters, which I didn't bother to read, and pictures, which I couldn't help but look at. They were taken out back by our pool, with Lynn in varying states of undress. She was in a bathing suit in some and naked in others. They were taken at night. I couldn't imagine when this was done or who had taken them, but I didn't really want to know any of this. I just wanted her out of my house.

Chapter Thirty-Four

Lynn stayed with Carol until she graduated, two weeks later. Then Joe called me with some surprising news. "Guess where the bitch is now?" he yelled through the phone.

I was dumbfounded by his tone. "Where?" I asked.

"At my father's. Can you believe it?" he yelled again.

"Calm down," I said. "What's wrong with that?"

"You won't believe this one. She told him that you abused her, stole all the money that she earned at the mall, and then threw her out," he yelled.

I almost jumped at him through the phone. "She said what?" I screamed. "How dare she? I stole from her? What does your father think?"

"He knows you better than that. Why do you think he called to tell me this?" Joe asked.

I told Joe I would go to see his father personally. I had not spoken to him since I took Lynn in, so I hoped he would receive me well. None of Joe's family ever bothered with me, even after I'd taken over raising Lynn, so I really didn't know what to expect.

I called my father-in-law to see when I could go to his house. I asked that he not tell Lynn I was coming because I wanted the element of surprise on my side when I faced her with her lies.

Lynn's face dropped when I came through the door.

I kissed my father-in-law hello and said a quiet hello to Lynn.

She walked out of the room.

Pop, as I called Joe's dad, said, "Come on back in here, hon."

I opened with, "Would you like to tell me the things you said about me in person?"

"I have nothing to say to you," Lynn said coldly.

"Did you tell your grandfather that you told me to kiss your ass before you left?" I asked.

"I never said any such thing," she said in feigned horror.

"Damn, you're good," I said. "If I didn't know better, I'd hate me too." I took my father-in-law aside and said, "Look, we're not going to get anywhere with this kid. I hope you know me better than all of this. I never hurt that child in any way. I only did what was good for her. If you're considering keeping her here, then watch your valuables. She's a thief. She'll take your money and your jewelry in a second. Watch yourself."

Pop gave me a kiss on the cheek and said, "My son did bad by you, and I'm sorry. I don't know what I'm going to do with this girl, but I believe you did your best. I want to thank you for the past two years of trying, even if Joey doesn't see it."

"He does," I said, and then I left.

Chapter Thirty-Five

I went home from my father-in law's house in a daze. When I told the kids that Lynn was gone for good, I was surprised at their resounding yell of victory. It was almost like, "Ding Dong the witch is dead." I couldn't believe my eyes or ears. It was then that I finally heard the horror stories of the mental torture Lynn had been inflicting on my children.

Eddie was then seven years old, and Katie, six. They told me how Lynn would hide from them while she was baby-sitting and stay hidden until they cried because they were afraid, thinking they were alone in the house. Lynn would frighten them by putting on white Halloween make up, and jumping out and scaring them in the dark. And the final horror was when she would call my line from her phone, make Katie answer it, and then tell her "The Boogey Man is coming to get you — run and hide." Katie would go fleeing to her room and hide under the covers.

I felt horrible, that she did such things to my babies, but I felt even worse that they didn't tell me when it happened. They said they didn't think I'd have believe them. After all, Lynn was a "big person," and I'd certainly believe her over them. So, I told them to never, never keep such things to themselves again. I hugged them and told them how much I loved them. I was determined never to let anybody hurt them like that again.

When I told Joe about the abuse, he wanted to kill Lynn. We knew she had emotional problems, but neither of us knew it was to such an extent, and neither of us thought it was simply because Joe was an absentee father during her formative years.

I called Lynn's mother to find out more about her. I told her what happened, and then I told her the stories I had heard about Lynn's abuse at the hands of her older step-brother. Lynn's mother assured me that there had been no abuse in her home. The only problem Lynn had was accepting Fred as her new step-father. The bloody eye, which I had been told was inflicted by Joey, had really occurred when she fell down drunk on the back porch the night she ran away. She had always wanted to be the center of attention, and with five new siblings, there was no chance of that.

I realized that the stories I'd heard about Lynn's prior home life were as real as the stories my father-in-law had heard about ours. Her mother's only lament was that she did not get professional help for Lynn when she saw the signs at an early age. She was truly a troubled young lady.

Two months later Joe told me Lynn snuck out of his father's house with all of her things as well as two diamond watches and a diamond ring that belonged to my dead mother-in-law. None of us have seen or heard from her since.

Chapter Thirty-Six

I was beginning to feel like a quadruped. After all, how many times can the "other shoe" fall on a two-footed person? I was, at the very least, surrounded by them. It seemed like I was destined to experience a skyful of falling shoes, but not without some really great times in between.

George and I went trippingly along in a very good relationship. We started our own business. He was excellent at home remodeling, so we opened a construction company. I still ran the trucking company with Joe, but since I worked at home, it was just as easy to run two companies as one from the same office. I handled his payroll and prepared his taxes for the accountant. It wasn't difficult since we only had two employees — George and me. On weekends I'd help him trim out houses. He taught me the ins and outs of how to cut molding at forty-five degree angles. I felt like a real jock when, with my tool belt on, I'd nail the boards into place. We did very well at the business for quite a while.

George was commissioned to build a house from the ground up. He got the blueprints, and sub-contracted out only the laying of the foundation and the roofing; everything in between, he did himself, with me at his side on weekends.

For nine months of the year, we only had my two children, and for the summers, we had his two as well. None of our friends could believe that we all got along so well. We often bragged that we never fought over anything, and, amazingly enough, we didn't. We agreed on all decisions regarding the children.

The closest George and I ever came to fighting was when we would go on our yearly vacations. George had a stubborn streak when it came to driving and other "manly things." Once, when we took the kids camping for a weekend, I had to laugh uncontrollably at his "me man, you woman" attitude. We had set up a rented pop-up camper at our campsite. George had tied the top of it to a tree to secure the top in an upright position. I had never camped before, so I didn't know why this had to be done, and quite frankly, I didn't care either. He just did it. That was fine with me.

After an absolutely freezing June weekend, in which the temperature dropped into the forties every night, it was, thankfully, time to break camp and leave. All the kids and I loaded our belongings into the back of the car, while George readied the camper to be reattached to the trailer hitch.

"Everybody ready?" he finally asked. "Did everybody make a potty stop?"

A resounding "Yes" came back at him, so George turned on the engine and we were off — or so we thought. Next came the sound of crushing metal. Our campsite neighbor started flailing her arms wildly in the air.

"What's her problem?" asked George, as he stepped harder on the gas. It felt like the car was suddenly a horse rearing up on its hind legs. You could almost feel the front wheels leave the ground.

George, clearly, had never untied the camper from the tree, and it was one strong tree. It wasn't going to move, and neither were we, in spite of George's effort at gunning the engine. The noise of the metal camper bending from the strain did not deter my macho man either. He was going to win this fight, and he gunned the engine for a third time. "What the hell? Are we in a mud hole or something? I can't move," observed Tarzan.

Finally, I realized why our neighbor was flailing like a wild woman. "You're tied to the tree," she was shouting above the engine's roar.

I started to laugh, and then George got mad. I'm sure he felt like a smacked ass, but I continued to laugh anyway. I jumped out of the car and turned to look back at the camper. It was a mass of crushed aluminum, but it was still tied to that tree. I doubled over in laughter. It looked so stupid, a car hitched to a trailer that was tied to tree.

George didn't see the humor in the situation. He got out of the car and didn't crack a smile.

The madder he got, the more I laughed.

When we returned the trailer to the rental place, the manager came out to inspect it. His faced dropped in disbelief.

"Did you take out insurance on this"? he asked, quickly flipping through his paperwork. "What did you do, roll it down a mountain or something?"

"Yes, we have insurance," George returned coldly. He didn't offer an explanation for the damage. He just signed the insurance papers and closed the contract.

We've never gone camping again.

Chapter Thirty-Seven

The next strain in our relationship came about, again, at vacation time. We booked a week's stay in a beautiful little resort in the Ozark Mountains, in Arkansas. When we told our friends that we were going to drive the entire 1200 miles instead of flying, they all said our days were numbered. After all, two adults and four kids trapped in a van for two twelve-hour days was putting patience to the test, not to mention that neither George nor I had ever driven across the country before. We supposed that if we could make it through that, we could make it through anything.

With George's patience behind the wheel, already documented, we were in for some real belly laughs. At least I was.

George had programmed the kids to make sure that they all went to the bathroom before we got on the road. They did. I, unfortunately, did not. So, his first test began only an hour into the first day when I asked him to pull off at the next exit. He did, begrudgingly.

Next, about an hour or so after we had made a lunch stop, the fast food we had all consumed decided to kick in. Little got a severe case of diarrhea. He was almost afraid to ask George to stop because he'd seen his reaction to me when I asked for a break. But, he finally did, again, and again, and again, for the next three hours of travel. We never made it past more than two exits without pulling off for Little to "leave a bit of himself" behind.

The second day proved to be much better. We actually made some time on the road. Once in the Ozarks, we set out to have a good week.

There were many different activities scheduled for teens and tots at the resort. There were dances and organized pool parties for the teens and trips to an amusement park and miniature golf for the tots. During the day, we would rent boats and fish, water ski and swim. I was in my glory. I floated around on a raft along side the boat and told George that someday we were going to live there. It was heaven on earth to me.

Eddie and Katie enjoyed all of their activities. Chris and Little, then sixteen and fourteen years old, were a bit more hesitant. Teenagers didn't mix well out of their element. I could not convince them to go to the dance. It's "so geeky," they said.

Chris was all too concerned with how the boys at the lake perceived her. She constantly combed her hair and asked if she looked all right. At sixteen, what's not to look all right?

However, one afternoon, after I had been out on the lake with her, Eddie, and Katie, I saw for the first time that Chris did not "look all right."

George and Little had rented a fishing boat for the entire day. I had rented the larger pontoon boat for a few hours. After some time, Chris, Eddie, Katie, and I went back to the van to go home. The van was parked in the hot sun, and its internal temperature was at least 110 degrees, if not more, when we got into it.

I put the key into the ignition to start up the air conditioning before we took off.

No air came on.

I attempted to put the windows down by pushing the power buttons.

No power.

I tried the radio.

No radio. The engine had started right up, but nothing else worked.

The temperature inside became unbearable. We could only open the vent windows in the back of the van about two inches, so we couldn't get much relief. So, up we went, on the mountain, to find a gas station.

It was only a two mile trip, but after we left the marina parking lot, I noticed that a light on the dash kept flashing "Check Brakes." I didn't say anything to the kids. I just drove like a snail up some hills and down others. We were all sweating profusely. I never knew I had sweat glands in my forearms before, but I found out that day. Even my elbow became so wet that it slipped off the arm rest of the seat as I drove.

I finally inched the van into the gas station parking lot, still tapping what I thought were bad brakes. When I came to a stop, Chris threw open the sliding door, bolted out of the van, and sat like a lumberjack on the nearest gas can. She proceeded to wipe sweat off of her brow with the tail of her shirt, while she was still wearing it.

The funny thing was not so much how she did this, but that she did it in front of a very cute, young gas jockey. For the first time, she did not "look all right." She looked comical.

I said, quietly, while laughing, "Chris, you look a bit unladylike sitting like that."

"I don't care. I'm hot. I don't care what I look like," she groaned.

I bought sodas for all of us and asked the mechanic to look into our problem. I also told him about the brakes. He checked out the fuses in the van and he found the one that was burned out. When he replaced it, the "Check Brake" light went out too. We were almost fried due to a seventy-five cent fuse. Needless to say, I purchased an entire box of those little suckers for future use. I also made sure he told me how to find them and replace them.

The week came to an end, and we set out for another two day drive home. My Honey, George, had been a sweetheart all week. We all knew, however, that this was about to come to an end. George was behind the wheel again.

Little didn't bless us with diarrhea this time, thank God. But we did, however, all have a very gassy meal on the road. The flatulence hit us all, except, of course, Mr. Perfect, who was driving. Since the van was closed up tight as a drum so we could benefit from the air conditioning, it became almost impossible to breathe from the smell.

"Jeez, what are you people made of?" he asked. "Does everybody have to fart at once?"

I started to laugh. "How can you control a fart, for God's sake?" I asked.

We couldn't very well ask him to pull over to pass gas, so we all lived with it for the next few hours. We chose to ride with the windows open and ninety-five degree heat blowing in on us.

When it came time for a dinner break, George pulled off at a stop marked with a food and gas sign. "We'll get some food," he said seriously, "but leave the gas here."

Then he proceeded to turn the van in the opposite direction of the food sign, heading straight for the gas instead.

We all looked at him, with the same bewilderment. "Hon, why are we going away from the food sign?" I asked.

He was still in his own world. He made a wrong turn, and he wouldn't admit it. So, he turned around in the parking lot of a lawn mower repair shop.

Eddie, not knowing any better, said, "This isn't a diner, Mom. They fix lawn mowers here. Why are we stopping?"

"Because I just wanted to check it out," George said through clenched teeth.

Next, he pulled into the gas station. I got out of the van as soon as I could to keep from laughing in front of him. I knew he was tired from driving for so long, and his patience was shot. But even the kids saw the humor in George's refusal to admit he'd made a wrong turn. I made it to the ladies room of the gas station just in time to keep from wetting my pants.

Chapter Thirty-Eight

Vacation over, it was time for the kids to go back to school. Eddie was then in third grade, Katie in second. Chris was a junior, and Little was a freshman in high school.

We took Chris and Little home to their mom's house after their summer with us. Billie, had relocated to a townhouse a few blocks away from her second ex-husband. Their marriage had only lasted two years.

It was quite a shock when, the day before Halloween, I got a call from Billie. "Hi. This is Billie. Is George there?"

"No, he isn't," I said, "He's still at work. Can I have him call you when he gets in?"

"Well, not really," she said, very timidly. "My phone doesn't work — my house just burned down."

Thump. There's the next shoe.

"You're house just burned down. Are you all right?" I asked. "How about the kids? Is anybody hurt?"

"No, we're all fine. We just don't have any place to go right now," she said. "The firemen just left, and all the stuff that wasn't burned is sitting out on the sidewalk in front of our house."

I told her to sit tight, that George and I would be down to get them in about an hour and a half. I had to call him at work, and then we arranged to take George's truck and my car down to Billie's house so we could bring them and what little possessions they had left back to our house.

We arrived to find Billie, Chris, and Little sitting on the curb in front of their burned-down house. They all seemed to be in shock. They were laughing and joking about the fire and how the firemen just left. I was appalled that no one had offered them any assistance, even so far as simply giving them directions to a shelter, or something.

Some neighbors were standing outside with them, but Billie didn't want to impose upon them by moving in, even for the night. So, this is how I inherited my Honey's ex-wife, his two kids, and their dog as housemates.

Chapter Thirty-Nine

When we got back to our house, we unloaded the truck and my car into the garage. Everything smelled of smoke, including Billie, the kids, and the dog.

We left the dog in the garage too, for several reasons. One, he was not properly house trained; two, Eddie and I are allergic to dog hair; and three, he was a Rotweiller, and even though he still wasn't fully grown, he was huge. Little thought I was terrible for keeping "poor little Brutus" outside, and he even shed a few tears over it.

Everybody took showers in an effort to wash the horrible smell off. I started to do some of the laundry that they managed to salvage from the fire. The clothes were wet from the water used to put the fire out. They saved a few of the kids' things because their bedroom doors had been closed and the fire went past those rooms. We had Chris's entire bedroom set, minus the mattress and box spring. Little was able to save his bedroom set too, as well as his stereo and weight training equipment. Billie lost all of her personal things because she slept downstairs on a sofa bed. The electrical fire started in the wall between the kitchen and living room, so all of that went up in flames. She had only the clothes on her back.

No one went to school the next day, due to all the excitement. Little joked about going out on Halloween as a fire victim. He wanted to blacken his face again and carry some of the charred remains we'd saved along with him to prove he had really been in a fire. Billie wouldn't let him do that.

Billie stayed with us for a week. Then she made arrangements with her brother, Bob, to move in with him and his wife. The kids stayed with us for three more weeks, since we had more room than Bob had in his apartment.

Once word got out that I was harboring a family of fire victims, the clothes started poring in. People from everywhere donated. Some people must have cleaned out closets that weren't touched in twenty years. We were given leisure suits, bell bottom pants, go-go boots, and baby clothes. You name it — we got it.   Finally, we had collected so much that I had to give what they didn't want to use to the Church Thrift Shop.

During Billie's week-long stay, I got to know her very well. I would spend hours at night talking to her, and I really enjoyed her company. I commented to George, "Gee, hon, I don't know why you divorced her. She's really nice."

"I didn't divorce her. She divorced me, remember?" he asked coldly.

"Oh, yeah, the mailman. I forgot." I said flippantly.

It hadn't occurred to me that George was uncomfortable around Billie, until he told me.

I asked him, "Do you mind that I have a friendship with her, even if you can't?"

"Knock yourself out," he said, "Just don't include me in on it."

I think George's attitude is why Billie made the plans with her brother as quickly as she did. But, in that one week, I learned a lot from her. For instance, I found out that she was psychic. She was both clairsentient and clairvoyant. She was able to feel the presence of, and sometimes even see angels or ghosts in any room she was in. She knew of a woman named Norma who followed her wherever she went. Billie told me that Norma had come to my house with her and the kids. I got the creeps. Billie, the kids, and the dog were one thing, but ghosts too?

"You know, you have the same ability. I can feel it."

"How could I?" I asked, "I don't feel anything. How would I know if I had it?"

"You just haven't tapped it yet. You have to be open to it. Let it come. You can't force it," she said.

Chapter Forty

Once Billie moved in with her brother, she enrolled the kids in the local public high school. She found a job nearby, and after a month, she learned of an apartment complex that had an opening. The only problem was that she had no money for the security deposit.

George and I gave her the money to get her back on her feet. We furnished the entire place — a kitchen, two bedrooms, and a living room — with hand-me-downs from everybody we knew. My parents gave them mattresses and sheets for their beds; my aunt gave them a coffee table, end tables, and lamps; and I gave her a queen sized sofa sleeper I had been using in my office. I had also, just months before, purchased a new kitchen set, and the old one was boxed up in my garage. So, she moved into the apartment, completely furnished, right down to the dishes and silverware, which my sister supplied.

Since they then lived in a neighboring town instead of so far away, George and I got to see the kids on a more regular basis. I would pick Chris and Little up from school and drive them to their apartment, since Billie was not home during the day to do it. Since they were older than Eddie and Katie, I would pick them up a few minutes later than my own kids. I became their daytime taxi, since I worked at home and had the ability to leave more easily than either Billie or George.

The hassle increased as time went by, however. Billie had gotten too far behind on her bills, and her car was repossessed. Then she became sick and had to be hospitalized, so we had to take the kids again. And, once Billie was out of the hospital, I took her to doctor appointments for follow-up visits.

One day, while sitting in the doctor's office waiting room, I heard behind me, as clear as a bell, my grandmother laughing. I turned around to see who it was, since Granny had been dead for twenty-five years. There was no one there. Not a soul. I must have physically jumped as I turned because another lady in the room looked at me strangely. I smiled weakly and turned back around. Then, without a doubt, I heard it again, just as clearly as the first time. Granny was giggling.

When Billie came out of the doctor's room, she smile slightly. I didn't say anything about the occurrence to her. I just got up to leave the office.

Once outside, she said, "There's an old lady near you. She's grinning from ear to ear."

"You can see her?" I asked, incredulously.

"Well, not see, like I see you, but I know she's there. Do you know who it could be?" Billie asked.

"Yeah, my grandmother. I heard her laugh twice while you were in with the doctor," I said.

"It's starting," Billie said. "You must be open enough for things to come through to you now. If you heard her laugh, then your ability is clairaudience. Your Grandmother is very happy with you. You must be something special to her. That's why you can hear her laugh."

Interesting choice of words, I thought.

I told Billie the story I remembered about Granny on the way home from the doctor.

"My guess is that your grandmother was psychic. But I also suppose that, being Catholic, she didn't act on it. She may have known you were destined to be the one who would come to know her best. I don't mean in this life, but in the next. I get the feeling that Granny is high up there with the Big Guy," Billie said.

I got the chills when she said that. "What do you mean, 'high up there with the Big Guy'?"

"I mean, she has some real pull. If you need something really badly, she's the one to go through to get to God," Billie said calmly.

"Wow," was all I could think of saying. A few minutes later, I asked, "How can I hone this talent?"

"Just let it come. It will. You'll be able to recognize it when it happens," she said.

Chapter Forty-One

I was suddenly very interested in dead people. I didn't have a death wish by any means, but I no longer feared it. The Catholic Church has always preached about life after death and seeing God, but, I was starting to actively research it. I read all the literature I could get my hands on about near-death experiences. I wanted to know what people saw when they crossed over.

I was extremely impressed with the movie, *Ghost.* When Whoopie Goldberg held Demi Moore in the form of Patrick Swayze, I thought, "That's perfect. That's what it must be like to be a spirit." And the way the good spirits were portrayed as white stars floating upward, and the bad, as black demons dragging you down, I got a real vision of the afterlife.

I didn't hear much from Granny for some time. I tried to hear her laugh, but I couldn't. I think I was trying too hard.

Then, one day, Mom had stopped to visit. She sat at my kitchen table, and we had coffee. Suddenly, I felt Granny in the room. It's hard to explain, but I felt her. It became clear to me that I was tapping my clairsentient ability at that point. I thought I'd take it a bit further. I said, in my thoughts, "Granny, make her feel you too." I said that over and over in my head.

Out of the blue, Mom said, "You know, I often wish I could go see my mother and father's grave. It's so far away, but I feel guilty for not making the trip."

I almost shit. I couldn't believe she said that. Both of my grandparents are buried in Arlington National Cemetery. The trip to D.C. takes about three hours, and she had never gone back after her father's funeral. And, then, after I sat there and begged Granny to "touch" her, Mom was suddenly talking about them. It was the neatest experience of my life, but I couldn't tell Mom what I'd done. I knew she'd think I was nuts.

I soon realized that the psychic power I had would show itself most often in the form of laughter. One morning around six o'clock, I woke up from a fitful sleep. I was unexplainably uneasy. I started to drift back to sleep when I distinctly heard the voice of Tony, Tommy's boy, call my name. "Mauween," the voice said, with a clear giggle. My eyes opened wide, and I looked around the room. No one was there of course. Again I heard, "Mauween," followed by a giggle.

I didn't know what to make of it. But I had an uncontrollable desire to get up and call Tommy. It was only six-thirty in the morning, and I told myself as I walked down the stairs to the kitchen that I shouldn't call Tommy at such an hour on a Saturday. But even as I kept thinking it was a stupid thing to do, I walked over to the phone. I thought about it again with the receiver in my hand. Then I dialed the phone.

Tommy answered the phone on the first ring. He didn't sound groggy. "Hello?"

"Hi, Tommy. It's Maureen. I'm sorry to call you so early but I have to tell you something," I said.

"No, problem, doll, I've been up for hours. I had another bad night; can't sleep much, you know?"

"Well, that's kind of the reason, I'm calling," I faltered. "I just had something happen to me and I thought I should tell you about it. I can't explain this and you may think I'm nuts, but I just heard Tony's voice as I drifted off to sleep. He was laughing and he kept saying my name; you know the way he did, 'Mauween;' but he was happy, Tom, he was really happy."

Tommy started to cry. "My God, thank you, thank you, thank you," he said through deep sobs.

"I'm sorry, I didn't mean to upset you. I thought it was a good thing and that you should know about it."

"It is a good thing, doll. Do you know how long I've waited to hear this? I was awake most of the night and all I can think about is how he died. I keep thinking about the pain he must have felt from that car smashing into him. I can't deal with the pain. And now you tell me he's laughing and happy. My God, this is what I've longed to know — that he's all right. Thank you."

Tommy never questioned me about my intuition. He was extremely happy to hear what I had to say, and accepted it. We said our good-byes and I went back to bed.

Chapter Forty-Two

Not long after that, Dad took sick. He had started to fall down while simply walking across the room. He wouldn't trip; he would just fall. He saw a doctor about it. After several tests, they discovered that he had a brain tumor located behind his left ear. It was affecting his balance.

They were going to operate on my father to remove the tumor, or at least the pressure it was causing, when more tests showed that he also had lung cancer. They decided to treat the cancer and, for the time being, ignore the brain tumor, since it had proven to be non-cancerous. He had to go twice a week for radiation therapy. My nephew, Jack, then a grown man of twenty-one, took him on Tuesdays, and I took him on Thursdays.

We had to hide my father's car keys from him because he was still under the impression that it was safe for him to drive. Here was an educated man who could not fathom our concern over his ability, or rather, inability, to operate a motor vehicle. Mom, my sisters, and I told him that he was a hazard to the rest of society when he got behind the wheel of a car. After all, if he couldn't walk without falling, he couldn't drive either. So, we all took turns driving him to the doctor for treatments.

Nancy, Retta, and I decided to throw a seventieth birthday party for Dad, when he reached that milestone. He was the first Gavin male in our family history to make it to that age. All of Dad's male ancestors had died between the age of fifty and sixty. The Gavin women, all, by the way, old maid aunts, lived to ripe old ages of ninety or better, but the men never made it that far — probably because they got married. So, on November 6th, 1990, we surprised Dad with a seventieth birthday party.

We had invited old friends of his from college days, as well as the entire Gavin clan. He came through the door, and was completely surprised, but he looked so frail. He was, by then using a cane to walk, and he stood by the door as everybody sang Happy Birthday, just smiling at us. I saw that he was weak, but still so proud. I knew he didn't have long to live. I was saddened at the thought in the midst of the jovial atmosphere.

During the next year, Dad's deterioration was very evident. I had ordered a wheelchair for him to get around. He still had power in his legs, but the falling was beginning to take its toll. He resisted at first, but then he gave in and got used to the wheelchair.

Christmas came around. Dad asked me and my sisters to do his shopping for Mom. He didn't want to go to the mall in the chair. Instead he called some of his old buddies, invited them over, and had a bottle of Scotch ready for them when they got there.

One afternoon, I was bringing Mom home from a shopping trip, and there sat Dad, drunk as a skunk, in his wheelchair. He looked so funny. His hair was disheveled, and he couldn't make his arm stay put on his arm rest. It kept slipping off, and he'd drop his head out of his own hand. Even sitting, he somehow managed to fall down. But, believe it or not, he was happy, and so were we. Mom and I both kissed him hello. He offered us both a drink. An Irishman to the end.

Chapter Forty-Three

Dad knew the end was near. He didn't talk about it much, and he certainly wasn't morbid about it. His younger, half-brother, Jim had died a few months earlier. At that time, he had said to me, "Ya know, Babe, I think I'll be seeing Jim and my mother soon."

I was surprised, not so much at him missing Jim, but at him missing his mother. Dad never knew his real mother, Loretta, very well. She had died of leukemia when he was four years old. His only sister, Kate, was two at the time. The one memory he had of her was that she had a beautiful singing voice. In fact, he always went to the eleven-thirty mass on Sundays because the singer at that mass sounded like his mother.

When Dad talked about seeing his mother again, I became sad at the thought of losing him. Since then, my brief research into the next world made me actually look forward to seeing Granny and others who had already passed away. I began to consider it a happy thing that Dad would finally get to see his mother after sixty-eight years.

We knew that it was a matter of days until Dad was going to leave us. We had, in effect, vigils by his bedside. Aunt Kate was there throughout the weekend. He had slipped into a coma and was burning with fever. He wanted to be home to die, so we only had medication for him, not hospitalization. Kate left his side and said that she would return the next day to see him.

Mom and I kept putting cold compresses under his arms in an effort to lower the fever. I tried to explain to him why we were freezing his armpits. I thought that he might be able to hear us, even though he was comatose. So, I talked to him about everything we did, as if he was perfectly alert.

Retta came in right after Kate left, so Mom and I went to sit in the living room with Retta. After a few minutes, I decided to go and check Dad's temperature once again. When I got to his side, he was pale and cool. He was gone.

Mom came in right behind me. She felt his head, and then she gently put her own down on his chest. She started to cry. I did not.

I looked up to the ceiling. I knew from my reading that when a soul starts to leave the body, it floats above the person. I supposed that Dad was still in the "floating stage" and that he could literally see us below him. I said, in my thoughts, "You can finally see your mom, now. Be happy."

I had the experience at that moment that my grandmother, who died at the age of thirty, was there in the room. She was reaching out to her son, who was physically seventy-two years old, to bring him home. I had a distinct awareness which I could not describe, but I could definitely feel the action in the room. Since souls are not bodies, Dad saw his mother as he remembered her, a young woman, and Loretta saw her son as the boy she left behind. She reached out to her four year old son, to take his hand, and they crossed over together.

After a time, we left Dad's side to call Nancy. She had not yet gotten there. She came over right away. Then we called the undertaker to come get Dad. It seemed to take hours for them to arrive. I called George to tell him. He said he already knew, that he had felt a coldness, a shiver, come over him about a half hour earlier. That was exactly the time I had found Dad dead.

After talking to George, I went outside to the backyard to have a cigarette. I sat on the step, and I finally started to cry. I didn't cry hard. Tears welled up in my eyes. And again, as clear as Granny's laugh, I heard Dad say, "I'm okay, Baby."

I heard that, not felt it, heard it. I knew Dad was going to be okay. The date was April 25, 1993, twenty-one years to the day after Carl died.

Chapter Forty-Four

We made the funeral arrangements in the next few days. Mom requested that all three of her sons-in-law and three grandsons be the pallbearers. That included George — even though he was not yet legally a son-in-law, Little, Eddie, and Jack. Eddie was only twelve years old, but he stood five foot, nine inches. He was certainly big enough for the job.

Once the funeral was over, we all returned to our daily activities. I kept hearing Bette Midler on the radio, singing *From A Distance.* I took great comfort from that song. One line says, "God is watching us, God is watching us, God is watching us... from a distance." I know that God is watching us, along with all of our loved ones who've gone before us... from a distance.

About a week after the funeral, I got a call from the school nurse that Eddie was sick and that he had to come home. I went to pick him up, and he seemed fine, but on the way home, he started to cry quietly.

"What's wrong, honey?" I asked.

"I don't know," he said, "I just feel like crying, and I didn't want to stay in school and be laughed at."

I asked, "Are you sad about Grandpop?"

Then he let loose.

I knew that was the problem. "You know, you should look at it as something to be happy about. He's with his mom, who he hasn't seen since he was a little boy," I said in an effort to comfort him.

Then, like a bolt, I heard my father's voice, "Aw, come on Ed, it's okay," coming from the back seat of the car.

I physically turned around to look in the back seat. I had heard Dad just as well as I could hear Eddie. It was very weird. I said to Eddie, "You know, I can practically hear Grandpop telling us he's all right. There's nothing to be sad about. We might not see him now, but we will some day. Don't cry, honey."

Eddie calmed down by the time we got home.

Chapter Forty-Five

A few months later, George and I got into a financial bind. The construction business wasn't doing very well. Our "off season" seemed to be stretching out too long. My paycheck was not making it by itself. So, we looked around for something we could do that would not interfere with our time schedules: a paper route.

I was slightly embarrassed to admit that, at forty-one years old, I became a college-educated paper boy, but honest money was honest money. So, every morning, George and I would get up at three-fifteen A.M. to go pick up our newspapers for a promised doorstep delivery time of five-thirty A.M.

It was September, and we ran around in the dark trying to find house numbers, which people didn't display very well. After a few weeks, we caught on to which houses were our customers. We carried flashlights so we would not be mistaken for burglars in the darkness. This, however, did not impress the neighborhood dogs. They would all commence barking the minute we entered their turf, and they wouldn't shut up until we left.

George and I had the route down to a science. He drove the car with a box of wrapped papers next to him in the front seat. I rode in the back, with a box of papers next to

133

me. He delivered on the left side of the street, and I delivered on the right. We sometimes made a bet out of who actually walked the farthest. He said he did. I said I did. We playfully argued for weeks that each of us was right and the other wrong.

Then I bought a walker's odometer. I wore it one night, George the next. I cheated the night I wore it, and I ran in circles or made giant S turns before I'd go up to a house to drop off the paper. I had to run because I didn't want George to catch on, which he would have if I had taken longer coming back to the car than usual. I clocked in at one and a quarter miles on my night. The next night, George clocked in at exactly the same mileage. So, either he ran in circles too, or he really did put on more miles than I did in a night. I never told him I cheated.

Then, winter set in with a vengeance. That was the year of "The Great Ice Storms" on the East Coast. It wasn't a fun time to be working in the outdoors. The roads froze over in early December, and didn't de-ice until mid-February.

One night, George was delivering his papers on the left side of the street, and me on mine. When I looked back to see why George hadn't picked me up, I saw the car sliding sideways down the street, with George in hot pursuit. He was not making very good time because he was sliding too, with almost every step, and the car was gaining momentum and getting away from him.

As usual, I started to laugh. Poor man. He's huffing and puffing after the car, and I just stood there and laughed. I decided to join him. I went to the crest of the hill, sat on the ground in the middle of the street, and started to follow George and the car down the hill on my butt. I was wearing a vinyl snowsuit, so I made the best out of a bad situation.

The car finally came to rest at the bottom of the hill when it hit the curb. George had given up on running and, by then, was walking to it. I came flying by on my ass right past him, screaming, "Wheeee" all the way down.

We actually had fun doing the paper route, although it reeked hell on our sleep habits, and although our love life took a dive because we were both too tired to even think about it. We were alone, with no kids to interrupt us, and we had real quality time during those wee hours.

After a year and a half, George and I were far enough out of debt that we could afford to give up the paper route. I actually missed it after it was over.

Chapter Forty-Six

The return to normal hours was a welcome relief. Our lives were on a routine track. But yet again, the next shoe was poised to fall.

I got a phone call from Billie. "Is George there?" she asked, far too reminiscent of the fire phone call.

"No, he's at work. What's wrong?" I asked, alarmed at the tone of her voice.

"Well, I have to talk to him. It's about Chris. But I want to tell him myself," her voice cracked.

"Tell him what? What happened to Chris?" I demanded. Her cryptic speech had my mind going in all directions — none of them good. In three seconds time I had Chris dead or severely injured in some horrible accident. "Tell me, Billie. Tell me what happened to Chris," I yelled into the phone.

She broke down and sobbed, "She's pregnant."

"Oh, is that all?" I said, not thinking. Since I had jumped to a deadly conclusion in that brief time, pregnancy was actually a relief. "I'm sorry," I tried to recoup, "I don't mean it that way, it's just that you scared the hell out of me. I thought she was dead, for God's sake, the way you talked."

"No, she's not dead. Just pregnant. What are we going to do?" she asked like a child looking for answers.

"We? I don't think we have too much say in the matter, do you? What does Chris want to do?"

"She's considering abortion. But she's really confused."

"How far along is she?" I asked.

"Two months."

"How about the boy, what's his story?"

"He loves her. He wants to get married. But she's so young," Billie's voice trailed off.

"Well, that's to be decided between her and the guy. What's his name? I didn't even know she was seeing anyone seriously."

"His name is Scott. He's twenty," she said.

"Great. George is going to want to kill him. A twenty year old with his seventeen year old baby. Do you still want to tell him yourself? Or should I soften the blow before he calls you?" I asked.

"Maybe you should tell him."

"Okay, I'll tell him when he gets in, and I'm sure he'll be right over to see Chris."

Chapter Forty-Seven

When George came in he was pleasant, as usual. He came over and kissed me on the cheek, as I stood by the stove preparing dinner. "How was your day?" I asked, stalling.

"Fine, hon, how about you?"

"Well, it wasn't so great. I got a call from Billie today. There's no easy way to say this, so bear with me. Billie called to tell you Chris is pregnant."

His face dropped. He walked over to the back door and looked out the window. "I told her to keep her legs closed, God damn it," he said, to my horror.

"Oh no you don't," I said. "You won't take that attitude with Chris. She may be stupid for not protecting herself, but she's no whore. She made a mistake. If you go over there with that attitude you'll lose her for life. Calm down. Think about Chris. She needs your support right now, not your condemnation."

"Well, she has to get an abortion. That's all there is to it," he said matter-of-factly.

"That's not your decision. The boyfriend wants to get married."

"Married? Who is this asshole, anyway?" George yelled.

"Hon, calm down," I said, putting my arm around him. "His name is Scott. He loves her. Give him that much. And," I added almost cringing, "he's twenty years old.

"Twenty-years old? I'll have the son-of-a-bitch arrested for rape," he yelled, flailing his arms.

"George, get a hold of yourself. You're not making sense. You have to calm down and think this through. Go over there and comfort Chris. She needs you now. Don't go off half-cocked and ruin your relationship. I'm not letting you leave here until I have your word that you won't say anything like that to her. Think it through, hon, this is her life we're talking about."

George's shoulders fell. He started to cry. Not full sobs, tears just fell down his face. I held him close and hard. "You know I'm right, hon. Go easy on her. She needs us on her side right now."

Needless to say, dinner was ruined for George and me. I put the food on the table for Eddie and Katie and called them to dinner.

George left to go see Chris.

Chapter Forty-Eight

Billie met George on the front porch. She begged him to keep his cool when he went inside. I had called Billie after George left our house to warn her of his foul mood. He told Billie he was fine and they went inside together.

Chris was in the living room with Scott. Scott walked over to George, hand extended, and said, "Hello, Mr. Bradford, I'm Scott, Chris's boyfriend."

George shook Scott's hand.

Chris ran into George's arms and hugged him hard. Her face was all red and swollen from crying. He couldn't say anything cruel to her when she greeted him that way. "Are you okay, honey?" was all he could ask.

"Yeah, I guess so, considering," she replied, nervously.

They all sat down. George was surveying the lecherous young man who had violated his baby girl. He wasn't all that lecherous after all, he noted. Just a normal looking kid. He asked Chris, "Okay, what are we going to do about this situation? You know abortion is the only way to go, don't you?"

"No, Dad, I don't know that. I don't think I want to do that. I still have time, and Scott and I may get married."

"Married? Chris, you're still in high school. How can you get married and raise a kid? You're too young, honey.

Think about your future. Do you really want to saddle yourself with a family so young?"

"I don't know. But I have to think about it — we have to think about it," she said, wrapping her arm into Scott's.

That's when George realized his baby was no longer a baby. She had declared herself and Scott a team, the only ones with any say about the problem they faced together. George sensed that, and decided he'd better not push it any further.

The rest of the evening was spent with George grilling Scott on how he would support his budding family. He wanted to know where Scott worked, where he lived, and generally everything about his family life.

George learned that Scott's mother had died earlier that year. He had two sisters and he was the baby of his family.

Scott's sisters looked after him as if he was still a kid. At twenty years old, he had to keep reminding them that he was a grown man. A week earlier he had gone through the same grilling from them that George was inflicting upon him that night.

After what seemed an eternity, George finally returned home. I was waiting up to find out how things went. When he got in, he was emotionally drained. He slumped down in a chair and rubbed his head. "She's going to do it," he said with a sigh. "She's going to have the baby. It's due June fifth."

"Oh, it's okay, Grandpop," I said, as I put my arm around his shoulder. "It'll all work out. She's a good kid. And she'll be a great mom."

Chapter Forty-Nine

It took no time at all for June to roll around. Chris gave birth to a bouncing baby boy on June tenth, graduated from high school on June seventeenth, and got married on June twenty-fourth. She may not have done it all in the right order, but she did it. She named her little boy Jimmy. He had blonde hair and blue eyes and looked just like Scott.

George, surprisingly, was quite the proud grandpop. He would go over to see Chris and her little family as often as he could. Scott had moved in with Billie, Chris and Little after he and Chris got married. So, the little family was not quite so little as one might think.

Billie was a doting grandmom. She was eager to help Chris with the new baby. She would take him for walks, while Chris caught up on her sleep. She would feed him without Chris asking. And she didn't even mind changing his dirty diapers. Billie was in her element. She loved babies and loved to care for Jimmy. This worked out extremely well, since Chris and Scott could both go to work while Billie took care of the baby.

Little, however, began to resent his mother's full attention to the new kid on the block. He had always been Billie's baby, and even at the age of sixteen, he was not mature enough to see the situation clearly. He felt that he was pushed aside to make way for the little intruder, who was in Grandmom's eyes, absolutely perfect.

After about ten months Little began to cut school. He would sneak out of the house at night and party in the woods with a bad crowd. He was in danger of failing his junior year of high school for lack of attendance. That's when Billie decided that Little would have to live with his dad. She figured that George could present more of an iron hand than she could, and Little would eventually learn to tow the line. She couldn't have been further from the truth.

Chapter Fifty

Little moved in with George and me permanently in September. He was enrolled in his senior year of high school and attended regularly. At least that was an improvement.

Little had never made a lot of friends at our house, and for a while that bothered me. He was an extremely outgoing kid, and I wondered why he never made the effort. I figured he was still adjusting to not being with his mom full time, and that time would heal all. George, Eddie, Katie and I still saw Chris, Scott and the baby regularly. Little didn't join us.

The school year passed quickly and Little graduated the following June. Chris, Scott, and Jimmy were at our house for the graduation party. It was at that party that Chris announced that she had joined the air force. Chris, Scott, the baby, and Billie were moving to Mississippi so she could train there.

George and I felt that this was a very positive move for Chris. We knew that we would miss her and her family very much, but it was an excellent move toward her future. Her life was going in the right direction and we were very proud of her.

It was not, however, good news to Little. I was sure he felt as if he was being abandoned by them. But he said nothing.

Little finally began to have some friends come around a few weeks after graduation. They all seemed to be nice guys. Some of them were attending to a local county college and showed great signs of maturity and direction. I was hoping that some of that would rub off on Little. But it didn't seem to.

Little got a job pumping gas. It forced him to keep long hours on the grave yard shift. He'd go to work at ten o'clock at night and finish at six in the morning. That was where his real trouble began.

The people Little worked with at the gas station were not the highest caliber of humanity. Their idea of a good time was seeing who could piss the furthest after a night of drinking in the woods. He had been working there for about two years when he was arrested for driving without a license, and having alcohol in the car. He was then nineteen years old.

Little had to go to court. He was given probation, fined three hundred dollars, and had his driving privileges suspended for six months. But he didn't seem to care. He kept going down a destructive path.

He was running with a bad crowd. He had several times in prior months, come home so drunk that he couldn't find his bed, and he'd sleep on the floor. Once he even slept in his own vomit.

These episodes were what brought George and me to our first serious arguments in our ten year relationship. I believed that Little was showing absolutely the worst example to Eddie and Katie. I positively would not tolerate his behavior going unpunished.

George, on the other hand, felt that Little was just feeling his oats or trying his wings, and opted to do nothing when Little behaved that way. All George would do, was make him clean up his own mess, thinking that was punishment enough. George and I disagreed on everything about Little's behavior.

One night Little came home so drunk, that in his stupor, he urinated all over the coffee table in the living room. When I came down in the morning to make the kids' lunches for school, I saw a puddle on the table, and Little asleep on the couch next to it. Eddie had left his English homework on the table, and it was soaking wet. I thought that Little had spilled a glass of water on the table, but I couldn't find the glass. I got paper towels to try to dry out Eddie's homework, when I noticed that I was blotting yellow water. I dropped the towel like a hot potato. I screamed at him, "Get up, you asshole!"

Little was groggy, but sat straight up, "What? What's the matter?"

"Look at this. You pissed all over the table. What the hell is the matter with you?"

He looked at the table. "I didn't piss on the table, Maureen. I don't know what that is, but I didn't do it" he said.

"It's piss, sweetheart. Want me to prove it to you," I yelled, as I grabbed the paper towel and held it under his nose.

Little lurched back in fear. He had never seen me so mad. It obviously frightened him. "I'm sick of this shit. If you have to be a fucking alcoholic, you're damn well going to be one somewhere else," I continued to rage on.

I woke George with my screaming. He came rushing down the stairs. "What the hell is going on?"

"Your son," I screamed louder at George, "pissed all over the table. Are you going to do something this time, or molly-coddle him some more?"

"Oh, shit. Little, what the hell is your problem?" George asked, totally frustrated.

"I'm sorry, Dad, but I don't know how that happened, honest," Little said with manipulative sincerity.

"Clean it up, son," was George's only reply.

I was furious, and the only thing I could do to calm down was to leave the room. I stormed into the kitchen. My mind was racing. I wanted to throw the little bastard out into the street. And I was getting dangerously close to wanting to throw George out with him.

Chapter Fifty-One

George was between a rock and a hard place. He loved me and he loved Little. He didn't want to have to make a choice between us. But his inaction was clearly driving me crazy. We would fight almost daily; it was always over Little, and one of his stupid antics. Little's next anti-social tendency surfaced when he took up lying for no apparent reason.

At that point, he was twenty years old. We had given him no curfew, and very few restrictive rules. We asked only that he call if he wasn't coming home for the night. For a short time that worked. Little seemed to respect the house rules and the heavy drinking seemed to subside.

But I soon discovered that Little was not going where he said he was. Once, he told us he was going to the Poconos for the weekend with his friend, Tim. Then Tim called our house looking for Little.

It was stupid for Little to lie to us. Neither George, nor I ever grilled him on his whereabouts, so we didn't understand why he felt the need to lie. This happened time and time again. Little simply lied about everything.

It all became crystal clear when Little came home from the gas station one morning. The station had a random drug testing policy. "Dad, I kinda, well I sorta, well, I got fired today. My drug test showed marijuana. It's all crap, Dad. Really, I mean, who doesn't do pot?" he asked arrogantly.

To my horror, George said only, "Son, you made a bad choice this time. Now you've lost a good paying job, and for what?" Then he left the room.

George's ability to keep calm in the face of turmoil drove me up the wall. I was livid. I stormed up the stairs behind George. The issue at that point was no longer that Little got fired for drug use; it was that George once again refused to backhand the little creep for his actions, or even more so, for his attitude. "Are you crazy," I yelled. Then the tears of frustration fell down my face. "I can't take this anymore. You have got to do something. Don't you see it's only getting worse?"

George turned to look at me. He had never seen me cry. I was angry and hurt. I didn't think I could continue to live that way.

"Please, please, do something, anything, to make that kid see he can't keep acting that way. You are only giving him your approval by not punishing him. Give him an ultimatum. Tell him he has to tow the line and follow the rules, or there will be a price to pay. And then, God damn it, follow through with it."

I slumped down on the step. I put my head in my hands and I cried hard.

Little came around the corner. He had never seen me cry either. Apparently, that's all it took. Little looked at me with tears in his eyes. "I'm so sorry, Maureen. I really am. I don't mean to be this much trouble to you and Dad. I don't want to see you two fight like this over me. Please, I'll straighten out, I promise."

I was moved by his sincerity. But I was suspicious of it.

"Little, you're going to have to do more than talk. You're going to have to live clean and sober. I don't know how far into drugs you are, and frankly at this point, I don't really care. But you will be the cause of your father and me breaking up, if you don't clean up your act."

"I'm not an addict."

"Famous last words," I said sarcastically.

"No, really. I was only doing pot on the weekends, and I'm really not addicted. I'll prove it to you. I'll stay home and not go out at all, you'll see."

Little stayed home every night for the next six weeks. He looked for work during the day, then he'd come home for dinner. He'd help me with the dishes, and he'd straighten up the house. He did the laundry, too. He was really making an honest effort.

We'd talk while we were doing the dishes. He told me that he felt lost and misdirected. He didn't know what to do with his life. He said he felt like he was a big disappointment to his father.

"You have disappointed him, Little, but you're not a disappointment," I said. "He loves you more than anyone in this world."

"You think so?" he asked hopefully.

"I know so," I said.

Chapter Fifty-Two

The weeks passed and Little found a few minimum wage jobs. He'd stay at each one for a short time, then he'd move on in an effort to find something better. But he wasn't having much luck. At least he had kept his word. He wasn't doing drugs or drinking anymore.

Finally, he came home one night and announced that he had decided to move to Mississippi with Billie, Chris and Scott.

George was taken back by the news.

Chris had just given birth to her second child, a girl, only three months before; to add Little to the mix didn't seem to be the best idea in the world. But Little seemed convinced that he could get a new lease on life in the south. Scott promised to help him find a job in the plant he worked in. And Chris was still home on maternity leave from her desk job at the Biloxi military base.

Little packed what meager belongings he had, and brought them down to the front door. He looked over at Eddie and Katie.

"Well, this is it, dudes. I guess I'm outta here."

He walked over to Katie and gave her a hug. Then he shook Eddie's hand. Finally, he came over to me. "I'll miss you, Maureen. I'll miss our conversations over dishes, too, believe it or not."

"You'll be fine, hon, take care of yourself. Try not to get discouraged. You can succeed if you try. Show some confidence. You've got a good head on your shoulders," I said, "use it." Then I reached over to kiss him goodbye.

George drove Little to the bus station and they said their good-byes there. Little boarded the bus bound for Mississippi.

Chapter Fifty-Three

There had been one bright spot during the three year trauma with Little that had helped me keep my perspective. Eddie, who was then sixteen years old, had decided to take flying lessons. He had gotten a job bussing tables and had saved enough money to pay for the lessons himself. I was very proud of his effort.

In his own way, Little had done me a huge favor. When Eddie and Katie observed his drunken antics, they were as disgusted as I was. They could see for themselves at a very young age, how stupid underage drinking was. It wasn't cool to them. They thought Little was a loser. They didn't want to do anything in life the way they saw Little do it.

So, when Eddie chose to fly, I backed him wholeheartedly, as did Joe. I would drive him to the local airport and I would sit in the car near the runway to watch as he and his instructor took off and landed time after time. It was very unnerving. But I knew the instructor, Steve, would not let anything happen and I took great comfort in that.

After a few months of this, I had complete confidence in Eddie's ability. I could see that his take-offs were improving, and his landings were less frightening to watch.

It was Steve's policy, not to tell any of his students when his first solo would take place. He figured that the student couldn't think about it overnight and become too apprehensive.

One beautifully sunny day, Steve went up with Eddie, had him make the normal circle pattern around the airport, and had him land the plane. Then he got out and said, "Today's the day, man. You're going to solo."

Eddie was ecstatic. He got out of the plane, bounded over to me in the car and said, "It's time, Mom, I'm going to solo right now."

My heart leapt into my throat. I knew this day was coming, but I wasn't ready for it. I didn't want to show Eddie my fear, so I said, with feigned happiness, "That's great, honey, good luck. I'll be right here watching you." He saw right through it, though, when I kissed him and hugged him with all my might. "I love you," I said.

"Mom, it's not like I'm not coming back. Relax," he said confidently. Then he turned and ran back to the plane.

I walked over to Steve. He had a radio in his hand. He held the radio out to me. "Do you want to talk to Ed when he gets up there?"

"Talk to him? I can barely watch this, and you think I'd be able to talk to him? No thanks," I said.

"He's fine. He knows exactly what to do. I wouldn't let him go if I had even the smallest doubt."

My baby was about to cruise down the runway in a tiny, single engine plane, with no one at his side. My heart was pounding. "Isn't it kind of windy today?" I asked Steve.

"It's fine. He'll be landing into the wind. There's no crosswind today," Steve said with a smile. I'm sure he had stood by many mothers who suddenly felt the wind was too high, or the plane too small. "Mothers," Steve said laughing and shaking his head. "My mom still has a problem watching me take-off."

"Well I guess I'm normal then, huh?"

"Absolutely. But seriously, he is an excellent pilot. You have nothing to worry about. Sit back and enjoy your son's accomplishment."

With that, Eddie's plane came speeding down the runway. He had normally used at least half of the runway before he got airborne, but this time, he was up in a flash, using much less than that.

"You'll notice that he went up sooner than usual. That's okay," Steve practically narrated the live action. "That's because I'm not in the plane. In small planes, the difference of one person's weight is substantial. He can get his speed up faster with less weight and take off easier. You'll also see that he will fly higher, sooner. He'll feel that right away, and he'll have to adjust his altitude."

Eddie did exactly as Steve said he would. He flew very high, very quickly. He also descended slightly when he became aware of it. I was aware Steve knew what he was talking about. But better yet, I was aware Eddie knew what to do. Very shortly, Eddie was in the circle pattern to land. I heard his voice over the radio in Steve's hand. He was speaking like a pilot. He said something I couldn't understand. It was numbers, and something about downwind. Steve explained that Eddie had to speak his location into the radio to announce that he was approaching the airport to land. Again, I heard more numbers from Eddie's voice on the radio, then the word, "final." That meant he was on the final approach to the runway. It notified any other planes in the area that he was coming in to land.

It was only a few more minutes, but it seemed an eternity, as I watched Eddie's plane come closer to the field. He was doing fine. I, nevertheless, was not. I had tears in my eyes when the tiny plane touched the ground. I was so proud, and so damn scared at the same time. But he did it.

My mind raced. *Mild cerebral palsy.* Those doctors were nuts. My boy was better than fine. He was healthy, happy, and damn good at flying that plane.

Chapter Fifty-Four

George and I still had to pick up the pieces of a relationship that only barely survived the trauma it had sustained. I had said some horrible things to him in my frustration over Little. His ego had taken a beating.

After years of telling him that he was inept at dealing with his son, I felt it was necessary to make him see how much I loved him.

Surprisingly, it was Joe who would make that possible for me. Joe came over to my house one afternoon for what I thought would be routine business.

After we had gone over some billing, he sat down on the couch opposite the desk. Joe didn't usually sit and relax when he was here, so I found that odd. He seemed to be settling in, when he said, almost nervously, "Don't you think it's about time we got a divorce?"

"About time? We've been separated for eleven years. I thought it was time twelve years ago. What the hell took you so long?" I asked, laughing.

"Well, I just thought we should finally take care of it. I looked into a place called the Divorce Store. It'll be real cheap, since we've got nothing to fight over. No lawyers are necessary. We just have to go to court and get it over with."

"The Divorce Store? What's that — a subsidiary of Divorces R Us?" I asked. "Sure, go for it. I'm game to finally call it a day. What do I have to do?"

"Nothing. I'll file. They'll give me some papers, to make things legal, we'll sign them, then we just have to go to court on the date they assign."

"Okay, let me know when you've got it all together."

Joe stood to leave.

I said, melodramatically, "Jeez, hon, what'll we tell the kids?"

He turned to look at me, shook his head and smiled, "I think they'll be fine."

When George came home that night, I gave him the good news. "You may be able to make an honest woman of me soon," I said.

"What do you mean?" he asked as he took off his coat.

"Joe wants a divorce. We can stop living in sin."

"No shit. What brought that on?" he asked.

"I have no idea, but I didn't argue."

"Well, I'll believe it when I see it," said George, doubtfully.

The next day, I got on the phone with a travel agent. I wanted to do something nice for George in celebration of my news. I decided to surprise him with a getaway weekend in the Poconos in one of those lusty resorts with mirrors on the ceiling and x-rated in-room movies.

We joined in the fun at the live stage show on our first night there. The emcee asked for volunteers to participate in a hula contest. I volunteered us.

First the ladies had to don grass skirts, line up, and dance the hula. Being a closet exhibitionist, I was in my element. I swayed from side to side in time to music. And, after turning it into more of a bump and grind contest, it was by audience applause that I was declared the winner.

Next up came the men. The emcee had taken them back stage, to also dress the part. He asked the men to remove their trousers, before putting on the grass skirts. We women were at least allowed to put them on over our own skirts. The men weren't given that chance.

George, however, was in the habit of not wearing underwear. And he didn't bother to mention this to the emcee. He simply put the skirt on, then removed his trousers. He figured he would be covered by the skirt.

The men were paraded out onto the stage. The emcee had made the ladies contest quite easy; music, dance, applause, that was it. The men didn't get off so easy. The music started much the same as ours had, soft and low. Then it was speeded up and the emcee encouraged the men to really get into it. He walked behind each contestant with his microphone in hand and spoke to each of them as they shimmied and shook. When the emcee reached George, he said, "Come on, pal, show us your stuff."

George did.

He shook so hard, the skirt fell down to the floor. There he stood, with nothing on from the waist down but his socks and shoes. The audience roared.

George quickly bent over to retrieve the grass skirt. He picked it up and tried, with little success, to cover everything. He managed to cover the front, but took no heed of his bare ass. The audience was hysterical. It took no time at all to declare George the winner.

For the rest of the weekend, whenever we'd go to the dining room for meals, George would get a standing ovation when he entered the room.

Chapter Fifty-Five

It took three months for the divorce paperwork Joe had filed to be assigned a court date. When the day arrived, Joe came over to my house to pick me up. We drove to court together.

While we were in the car, I opened the big manila envelope to see exactly what I would be signing. It was pretty standard stuff. I would have custody of the kids; Joe would pay child support; the business would remain the same, and no property would change hands. All of those things had already been taken care of simply by the passing of eleven years.

I did find one detail that was either a typographical error or Joe had given the Divorce Store the wrong information. It proved to be Joe's mistake. He was never good at details. I laughed when I read the birth dates of the kids. Eddie was listed as born on December 14, 1980, and Katie was listed as born on January 27, 1981.

"God, I'm good," I said to Joe as he came to a stop light.

"What?"

"I gave birth to two kids only one month apart, according to this," I said.

"What? What are you talking about?"

"That's what it says, Joe; Eddie in 1980, and Katie one month later in 1981."

"Oh, who cares," he said flippantly. "The judge won't give a shit."

We arrived at the court house at seven-forty-five in the morning. Our case was scheduled to be heard at eight-fifteen. By eight-thirty, Joe and I sat before the judge.

The judge told Joe he had to read into the record everything that was on his copy of the documents. Then he added, before Joe could speak, "Mr. Walker, I think you might want to make a correction before you start to read. The dates of birth for your two children do not appear correct, unless of course, one or both of your children are adopted."

"Hah," I said a bit too loudly, as I nudged Joe.

"Yes, you Honor, there is a mistake. The year for the second child should be 1982, not 1981."

The judge saw my action, and smiled. "I must say, I wish all my divorce cases were this easy. You two seem to have it together. I see here you've met the state standard of eighteen months of separation, and exceeded it by more than ten years. I suppose there is no chance of reconciliation?"

"No, your Honor, no chance of reconciliation."

"Fine, read your statement, sir," said the judge.

Joe read the statement into the record. When he was done, the judge looked at me. "Do you contest this action, Mrs. Walker?"

"No, your Honor," I said.

The judge pounded the gavel. "Divorce granted. You may pick up your final decree in thirty days, at the clerk's office, or it can be sent to you. Which do you prefer?"

"You can send it, your Honor," said Joe.

"Fine. Next case, please."

That was the official end of our twenty-two years of marriage.

Joe and I left the courtroom and went out to the parking lot. When we got to the car, Joe opened the door for me. "Wow, is that what divorce does? You never opened a door for me when we were married," I said sarcastically.

"Shut up, or I'll go back in there and tell the judge to marry us again," Joe said.

Chapter Fifty-Six

In the summer of 1997, George and I took Eddie, then sixteen, and Katie, fifteen, back to my "little heaven" in Arkansas.

Eddie and Katie had been going with us every year. But our family size had dwindled with the marriage of Chris, and with Little joining her in Mississippi.

My kids, unlike Chris and Little, liked to join in the scheduled teen activities. In fact, they had been doing so since they were in the tot's program, years earlier. The resort still ran dances, miniature golf nights, and pool parties for the teens. But the activity Eddie and Katie liked best was the afternoon on the lake with jet-skis.

The day camp counselors would pile all the teens on a pontoon boat with jet-skis in tow. Then they'd motor out to the center of the lake, and let the kids take turns riding them.

That year we had scheduled a two week stay. So, that meant that every activity Eddie and Katie signed up for in the first week, they could also sign up for in the second week as well.

It was during our first week stay that news came over the television one night, that a twenty-three year old man had drowned in the lake. He had been with his family on a pontoon boat, when his father's hat blew off in the wind. The young man dove off of the boat to retrieve the hat. The boat had been traveling quite fast, so that was not the brightest thing to do. It was not known then exactly what happened, but obviously something went wrong, because the young man never surfaced. It seemed quite a sad story.

Then, as the days went by, stories circulated around the marina that perhaps it wasn't an accident. Apparently, the young man was largely in debt and it was speculated that he may have faked his own death. At least that was the rumor. However, they never found a body. So for the rest of the week, we irreverently joked that we should watch out for the dead guy, whenever we were on the lake. George asked at the marina where this accident occurred, so he could reassure us that we'd stay upstream from the sight. None of us wanted to be the one to discover the dead guy after he was under water that long.

On the second week of our stay, the kids were once again on the teen jet-ski outing. Katie was about to climb onto the jet-ski when she asked, over the roar of the motor, "Hey, have they found that dead guy, yet?"

The counselor almost choked. The kids on the trip that week hadn't heard of the accident, and the counselors thought it best not to let them know there was a body, possibly somewhere in the area. The counselor asked Katie to get off the jet-ski. "I'd appreciate it if you would keep your voice down. We don't want to scare anybody," he said to her, quietly.

But it was too late.

"Dead guy?" asked another girl quite loudly.

"What about a dead guy?" asked yet another kid.

The secret was out. The counselor had to explain to the rest of the group about the mishap the week before. He stressed, in his version, that the guy probably faked his own death and wasn't even in the lake at all. Some of the kids decided against going in the water in fear of bumping into the dead guy. Others, wanted to get out the snorkeling equipment and see if they could see the dead guy on the bottom of the lake.

When the outing was over, Katie and Eddie came back to the marina. George and I were waiting on the dock to pick them up. Katie rushed up to me with a most indignant attitude, "Mom, I got in trouble for talking about the dead guy," she said. She'd said it so fast, that all I understood was, "the dead guy."

"What? Slow down. Say that again."

"All I did was ask if they found the dead guy yet and Cory, that guy over there, yelled at me for telling everybody," she said in one breath, while pointing accusingly at the counselor.

"Calm down, Katie," I said laughing. "It's no big deal. It's probably not too good for business to admit there's a dead body in the lake."

She was not deterred in her indignation. She wanted me to go over to the counselor and reprimand him for his treatment of her. I put my arm around her. "It's okay, honey. He didn't mean anything personally, I'm sure. They just don't want it known — no big deal."

The very next day, the dead guy surfaced. The story hit the papers and the nightly news. Katie was vindicated. At last, everybody in town knew the whole story, and Katie wasn't responsible for them knowing it.

Chapter Fifty-Seven

Katie was just beginning to come into her own. She was an athletic, happy, young lady. She had been cheerleading for the town's football team since she was twelve years old.

She tried out for, and was accepted on the junior varsity team during her freshman year of high school. It turned out to be quite a disappointment, though, when the JV girls were constantly treated as second class citizens in school. They were never allowed to take part in pep rallies, and all of the fund raising that they did, went toward the varsity team's uniforms or competition fund. So she was often frustrated.

In Katie's second year, though, she tried out for the varsity team. Once accepted, she was on cloud nine. At least she would gain some respect, or so she thought. But that was not to be, either.

The varsity girls were a fiercely competitive bunch. Instead of acting as a team, and showing the comradery of team spirit, they were the most selfish and downright malicious bunch of young girls I ever had the misfortune to meet. And Katie didn't handle it too well.

It turned out, that after six months of back-biting, cat-fighting, and general obnoxious behavior on the part of the cheerleading squad, Katie discovered that her beloved sport, was not so beloved after all. She gave it up one month short of finishing the season. Not one to be a quitter, her spirits fell.

Katie was very mature in many ways, but in this instance, her innocence surfaced. She honestly believed in the goodness of people. When she saw the girls behave in such a mean spirited manner, she didn't understand it. But she knew she wanted nothing to do with it.

So, Katie trained her sights on something new. She saw an advertisement on television touting a model search in the area. She wanted to try out for it.

She was certainly pretty enough. She had long, very silky, brown hair. She stood five feet, seven inches tall, and was very thin.

My apprehension was fear of the industry itself. I'd heard too much about drug use, wild people, and basically, a very fast life. If Katie had a problem with bitchy cheerleaders, then modeling, in my opinion, would really open her eyes to the cruel world. I wasn't too happy with this choice of career for my little girl. And Joe wasn't too happy with the idea either.

But, as Katie pointed out, Joe and I had let Eddie follow his dream when he took up flying. Perhaps we should consider thinking that one through a bit more, she had suggested. Joe and I relented; and Katie and I went to the audition.

As luck would have it, she was chosen from a room of two hundred people. I was happy for her. Her self esteem soared.

I enrolled her in modeling school. There she learned how to walk on a runway, style her hair by herself, and do her own make-up. Much to my surprise, the other young girls she met at the school were a far cry from the cheerleaders. They were helpful to each other with beauty tips, and even offered to exchange clothes for the runway sessions if someone didn't have the right outfit. She quickly became an expert at hair and make-up. She had never been one to wear a whole lot of make-up, so the first time she made herself up at home she exclaimed, "Jeez, Mom, I look like a hooker."

"No you don't, honey, you're just not used to it. You actually look very nice," I said.

Then she went downstairs to show George.

"Good Lord. You look twenty years old, girl," George exclaimed. He looked at me with raised eyebrows.

"Doesn't she look nice?" I asked him, pleading with my eyes that he not say anything negative.

"Nice, yeah, but a whole lot older," he said reading my face.

It was true that Katie aged herself when she wore make-up. Her natural beauty actually astounded me. I guess all I had ever seen was my baby. But when she was done up so artistically, I saw a beautiful young woman. It surprised me; but it unnerved George. "Hon, she's gorgeous. I don't think she'll have a problem getting an agent when the time comes. Do you think you're ready for New York and all that goes with it?" he asked.

"I'll worry about that tomorrow," I said.

For her young years, Katie was surprisingly mature. She knew that modeling, while an excellent career, would not be enough to sustain her. The school stressed that the girls stay in high school, and even go on to college if possible, because modeling, at best would only supplement an income. Most girls would never make it to the big time and instead would have to settle for some small photo ads or an occasional fashion show.

Our next item on the agenda was to get a portfolio together. She had both black-and-white and color photos taken.

She, indeed, photographed much older than she was. She was extremely photogenic.

By the time the portfolio was completed, Katie had turned sixteen. She hadn't found an agency to represent her, so she looked in other directions.

Katie knew she had to keep her grades up in high school, because she intended to major in business in college. She was diligent in her studies. And she started working toward her goal. She took a job at an accounting firm, doing filing and data entry. That way, she could get a business background before she entered college, and she could pay for the costs of her budding modeling career at the same time. Make-up and clothes were not cheap, and she wanted to do it on her own.

My baby was growing up in front of my eyes. Although my heart could burst with pride in her achievement, I was afraid to admit, tomorrow was getting closer.

Chapter Fifty-Eight

George and I scheduled a trip to Arkansas in March of 1998, specifically to look at property. I had always said I wanted to live there, so we bought some ground. The property is on a golf course, and it overlooks a small pond. It is simply beautiful.

We decided to build our own house. We agreed on floor plans for a nice little rancher with three bedrooms. The entire back of the house will be windows, so we can look out at the pond. We'll have a deck on the side and back, so we can sit by the golf course. I suppose this means I'll have to take up golf in my old age.

Everyone has settled down for the time being. Chris had baby number three, another boy, in January of 1998. She's made a career in the air force for the last five years.

Little has been a clean, sober, productive member of society for two years.

Eddie is about to embark on a college career that will take him to the sky — literally. He's going to major in aeronautical science, with the hope of flying for a major airline when he graduates.

And Katie, well, she's still hoping to be the next Cindy Crawford. I believe she can give old Cindy a run for her money, too.

Even Joe straightened out his life. He stopped gambling and got remarried for the third time to a wonderful lady who is a great step-mother to my children.

George and I haven't gotten married yet. We figure if we've managed to stay together for twelve years, through thick and thin, there's no sense in tempting fate.

I look forward to growing old with George in Arkansas. My life has been replete with falling shoes. But since I'm only at the ripe old age of forty-six, I'm sure there will be more shoe storms to come. I've managed to survive so far with only minor cuts and bruises. I'd say that's not half bad. Wouldn't you?

About the Author

Maureen Gavin is a 1974 graduate of Rutgers University. There she majored in English with a minor in journalism. Her writing career got sidetracked for many years while she lived her life, and inadvertently compiled material for her first book.

While Ms. Gavin raised her children and held jobs as menial as delivering newspapers at four o'clock in the morning, and as heady as owning and operating her own corporation, she never lost sight of the book she would put down on paper one day. She filled the gaps by writing a newsletter for a volunteer organization, and faithfully kept her journal on an almost daily basis.

Ambitious and goal oriented, Ms. Gavin pursued every aspiration with a positive outlook. Every time she was knocked down, she came back up, stronger for the experience.

www.ingramcontent.com/pod-product-compliance
Lightning Source LLC
Chambersburg PA
CBHW020422290526
45785CB00002B/679